THE SERVICE STARTUP

DESIGN THINKING GETS LEAN

A PRACTICAL GUIDE TO INTEGRATE
DESIGN THINKING AND LEAN STARTUP

"I'll admit it: I enjoy seeing someone who knows their stuff re-assemble and improve on the work of an adjacent profession. Tenny calls out what's lacking in the Lean Startup approach, in the most thorough and insightful ways. In the spirit of iteration, he's taken an existing approach and improved on it. If only all criticism were this good. I enjoyed his delightfully nuanced views on the world of services — how they're perceived, experienced, and remembered — as well as his historical perspectives on the worlds of design, business and marketing. Opinionated but also well-informed, this is a pragmatic, human-centric take on designing and delivering services that I'd recommend to anyone whose work affects other people."

- Chad Thornton

Experience Designer :: Airbnb.com.

"To my beloved wife Tais Pancier."

ACKNOWLEDGEMENTS

My journey toward applying design to startups remains full of challenges, great encounters and wonderful collaborations.

I would like to thank my team at Livework for helping me prove my theories against complex business scenarios. Thank you for validating many of the concepts discussed in this book.

My gratitude also goes to the Eise community, including its students and startups, for the many learning opportunities I had while mentoring them over the last two years. The development of an acceleration program through design demanded a long road of experimentation and adjustments until it reached the maturity level necessary to make into this book.

A special thanks to Servicedesignsprints.com, its team and community of sprint masters. Servicedesignsprints.com is a movement born out of the desire for service design to be accessible for all.

Not related specifically to this book, but to my whole journey in life, a special thanks goes to my mentor and business strategist Yoda João Batista Ferreira. Our paths crossed early when I was young, and our long and profound conversations since then have helped me forge my strategic thinking and holistic perspectives. That made me a better designer.

I would also like to extend my gratitude to Ben Reason and Lavrans Lovlie, authors of *Service Design—From insight to implementation*, Livework founders, and fathers of the commercial service design practice. Thanks for the trust and partnership all those years.

Last but not least, here are some friends that are also part of this journey: Kerry Bodine, Mauricio Manhães, Rafael Vasconcellos, Jose Mello, João Belmont, Gustavo Bittencourt, Denis Russo, Mario Fioretti, Lincoln Seragini, Adilson Chicória, Camila Santos, Ivan de Marco, Karina Canêdo, Danyelle Iamada, Josh Levine, Angela Yeh, Mel Lim.

CONTENTS

STARTUPS, BUSINESS AND THE HUMAN SPECIES

As a future enterprise takes its first steps, the customer does not exist yet—although some schools of thought consider someone who still has not made a purchase to also be a "customer." Collectively, we are very connected, and most young people in consumer societies want to be "entrepreneurs." Large corporations have already realized this, and investors have organized themselves to try and win the lottery of the newest-idea-turned-into-successful-business.

In this Startup era, every company's beginning is visionary and lean. A man's new business venture is merely another form of the same creative manifestation that started with human migrations from Africa about two hundred thousand years ago.

It was, however, by the end of the fifteenth century, with the expansion of colonialism through navigation, that our species came into contact with other diverse groups. Before this time, these groups had been isolated for thousands of years. Europeans invaded cultures in the Americas, Africa and Oceania, decimating, ruling and subjecting other peoples to their perspectives…it all spelled domination.

The next great breakthrough came with the Industrial Revolution. We sorted out power, travel and task repetition—and we learned to fly, even beyond the stratosphere. Industrial design emerged, harmonizing functionality and aesthetics for mass production. We were collectively enchanted by robotics, both on a macro and on an infinitesimal scale, by space travel and by nanotechnology's manipulation of molecular structures. Scientific work is no longer the expression of isolated individuals. Rather, it is the fruit of intense collaboration between allied groups seeking to comprehend phenomena and synthesize substances capable of "curing" our illnesses, thus increasing life expectancy.

As for the expansion of our presence in the world, about two hundred thousand years after the migratory journey from Africa, at the dawn of the twentieth century, we achieved the landmark of one billion people. Just one hundred years later, the world's population reached an astonishing seven billion people—seven billion mouths to feed, seven billion thinking brains.

In the first few years of the twenty-first century alone, the human population grew by over one billion.

Following the vertiginous growth of urban populations, we have rapidly evolved into a world of services. One in which new "prosthetics" connect our minds with handheld tools, thus achieving the most challenging step of all: the simulation of thought itself.

Fortunately, in the cacophony of so much information, we can utilize the design approach as a basic toolkit of interconnected human actions for problem-solving. Expertly designed services are creating better environments to live, reproduce and nurture ourselves.

The journey of our species follows along this evolutionary path where science works increasingly hand-in-hand with design. Our comprehension and awareness as we participate in the connected world will generate intense empathy and collaboration, enhancing our perception of proximity in today's reality.

As some experts have shown us, the more we utilize design's perspectives, which are oriented toward serving the human species in harmony with the scientific point of view, the more efficient the protocol for creating companies that provide truly innovative services will be.

Tenny's book is a lantern on the bow, showing us how to orient ourselves for this colossal task of developing new companies that provide innovative services while nurturing respect for nature. Today's startups will become ever more humanized and beautiful.

João Batista Ferreira

UN director for the Eco-92 global sustainability forum and head of institutional relations at Eise - The School for Service Innovation.

THE CONCEPT

Part One

THINKING, THOUGHTS ON DESIGN

—————

Chapter One

*"Design is not just what it looks like and feels like.
Design is how it works."*

— Steve Jobs

Life was difficult for people moving into cities during the Industrial Revolution. Rural mechanization and the arrival of factories completely upended the traditional work routine. A typical day in the factory was full of repetitive, arduous tasks and could last for more than 14 hours.

When we look back at the Industrial Revolution, we can track the origins of the production processes that evolved to become Lean practices and ultimately served as inspiration for the Lean Startup methodology, a rapid development approach largely adopted by startups today. But what many do not know is that design was born at that very same age, out of the same influences, struggles and technological advances brought by the mechanization of humankind. As siblings sharing the same mother, they of course have their differences. One is scientific, extremely rational, while the other is humanistic, empathetic and has a soft heart for emotions. Both attitudes are needed in the making, so, in the end, it is not really a matter of choice between the two approaches. There should be no science without empathy, and innovations are only good if they leave the sketchpad.

During the first decades of the Industrial Revolution, production became the only concern for businesses. And much like today, performance was a huge marketing differentiator. Companies with the ability to produce more goods, quicker and cheaper, had a key edge. Considering the pressure to perform, human rights in the work environment were non-existent and employees were reduced to part of the production machine.

With the historical importance that we give to the Industrial Revolution in the study of business dynamics, one can be misled into thinking that people have always been subject to only learn and execute the work routines enforced by giant corporations. But this is just untrue.

Back before the smoky days, artisans used to dominate the commercial landscape and the work and learning routines for artisan workers couldn't be more different from the ones factory workers performed after the advent of the Industrial Revolution.

On one hand, artisans had a meticulous and mindful construction routine that entailed a deep understanding of materials and production process, mastering a range of relevant crafts that were passed down between generations. On the other, the factory workers had no legacy to pass on, nor did they have a vision that would allow them to better understand the purpose of their work. Considering the monotonous tasks and the poor work conditions of the factories, employees were literally showing up to work their bodies, leaving their minds and souls elsewhere. Fordism emerged from this dismal scenario.

Fordism is a movement that gained its name after Henry Ford, the creator of assembly lines and the intellectual father of mass production, and it can be described by three aspects that illustrate the work dynamics of factories during the rise of the industrial age:

1. The standardization of products (nothing hand-made: everything is made through machines, molds and unskilled labor, not by skilled craftsmanship)

2. The use of special-purpose tools and/or equipment designed to make assembly lines possible: tools are built to allow low-skill workers to operate "assembly lines" where each worker performs the same task over and over and over again.

3. Workers are paid higher living wages, so they can afford to purchase the products they make.

The benefits of the economic developments and increased living standards brought by the Industrial Revolution are beyond question. However, its new social dynamics reshaped life as we knew it. One clear example is the split between work and purpose.

It was like the apple had been bitten, and now there was no relation between people's sense of purpose in life and the work they did every day. Instead, people spent hours performing mindless tasks in exchange for wages. This new, imposed separation meant people no longer connected work with pleasure and this ended up leading to the separation between work routines and creativity.

The human instinct for creativity is fully connected to people's perception of growth and contribution. These two basic human needs are essential to achieving the flow state, a mental state of concentration or complete absorption proposed by the Hungarian psychology professor Mihaly Csikszentmihalyi, which is proven to be a highly creative state of mind. Unless one believes that they are part of something bigger—learning and growing in the process of discovering the world or themselves—there's no desire, or even space, for creativity to be triggered.

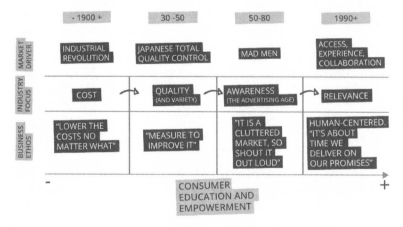

This absence of creative thinking was not a problem in the very beginning of the Industrial Revolution, as man was needed only as a part of the machine. In recent decades, however, with the shift of the focus from technological to human-centered innovations, production capacity and quality management alone became no longer sufficient to grant businesses a competitive edge.

The first instance of Design as a way to spark humanism and creativity within the industrial sectors dates back to the Bauhaus era. The transdisciplinary school founded in Germany in 1919 by Walter Gropius preached that the new, efficiency-driven scientific production methods were not enough to prepare industries to create things that people would desire, love, and cherish for.

"The common error today is that usually questions of efficiency are viewed from the technical and profit standpoint, without regard to organic considerations. The Taylor system, the conveyor belt and the like remain mistakes as long as they turn man into a machine, without taking into account his biological requirements for work, recreation and leisure."

- Moholy-Nagy, painter, photographer and Bauhaus professor (1938).

According to professor Nagy and other Bauhaus leaders, there was urgency for a new breed of professionals. These people would be able to bridge the arts and other humanistic disciplines with industrial production practices. Leonardo da Vinci, with his gigantic efforts and superhuman achievements, was the great example of what could be reached with the integration of art, science and technology. Bauhaus leadership claimed that only such a professional would be able to empower the industry to fulfill the needs and expectations of a more sophisticated and demanding consumer.

Gropius preached that in order to make this shift, the industry needed to look back to primitive humans, who out of necessity were masters of their own crafts. According to the Bauhaus, industrial leaders also needed to learn from the era of artisan practices, where there were a mix of arts and handcrafts. This was not a call to go back to the old workshop, but to find inspiration and create new approaches capable of incorporating multi-disciplinary human values into manufacturing practices. The industry would then liberate the potential for creativity, enabling the production of real social and economic value.

In contrast with the Arts and Crafts movement that emerged in opposition to the Industrial Revolution and its technological advances, Bauhaus leader Walter Gropius, along with the Hungarian artist Moholy-

Nagy, believed this new breed of professionals should rise from a collision between the humanistic and technological disciplines. Their vision culminated in the construction of an intellectual discourse capable of combining the works of photographers, engineers, artisans, fine artists, architects and the like. Thus, the first Industrial Design School was born.

Let's pause for a moment. When I say Bauhaus was the first "Industrial Design School," I could easily replace the word Industrial with the word Business. In 1919, to be in business meant to have an industrial production facility.

Had everything worked as Gropius, Moholy-Nagy and other Bauhaus leaders planned, we would now have design taught not as a specialized profession, but as a set of abilities, skills and, mainly, a way of thinking, relevant to business and well-suited to be integrated with all professions.

By understanding the history of the Bauhaus pioneers, it becomes reasonable to state that the integration of design into business and production methods is not new. Neither it is a recent trend. Contrary to that, business relies on the very essence and purpose of design, which is to empower the industry to generate social and economical value. Design is therefore a crucial part of business that was lost over the years.

*"**Designing is** not a profession but an attitude. Design has many connotations. It is the organization of materials and processes in the most productive way, in a harmonious balance of all elements necessary for a certain function. It is **the integration of technological, social, and economical** requirements, biological necessities, and the psychological effects of materials, shape, color, volume and space. **Thinking in relationships**".*

- Laszlo Moholy-Nagy.

The Bauhaus was closed down by the Nazism movement, and in the decades following the term "design" took on an aesthetic connotation. This is not to say that aesthetics had not been an important part of the design practice before. It was, and always will be. Would you choose an uglier model if price and quality were similar?

"When I am working on a problem, I never think about beauty but when I have finished, if the solution is not beautiful, I know it is wrong."

- Buckminster Fuller.

The problem was that while aesthetics were an essential part of good design (out of many), it slowly engulfed the whole field. This repositioned design as an artistic practice.

During the '40s and '50s, having a production facility became ubiquitous, a mere commodity. Companies looking to better position themselves in an increasingly cluttered market needed to be creative. In order to incorporate creative practices into their making, modern organizations hired external help. They turned to an external, ad-hoc, creative brain: the advertising agency.

With the widespread and increasing strategic influence of advertising agencies—arguably the main contractors of designers in the new information era—designers were put aside, away from working on function and other business-relevant issues and toward the aesthetic aspects of the making process. In doing so, the design practice gravitated toward form and beautification, leaving strategic decisions to engineering, marketing and administration professionals. It was not up for designers to dictate how things would behave anymore.

Since educational systems are informed by existing socioeconomic structures, the focus of design education also moved toward filling the demand for designers with aesthetic training. Over time, design drifted from an attitude of problem-solving toward a specialized and shallow profession.

That's how it became normal to think only of aesthetics, form and beauty when we hear the term design. This is a common assumption that is still prevalent today.

Looking back to earlier definitions and practices of design allows us to explore possible synergies with scientific production approaches. Nowadays, as Lean Startup and other Lean Manufacturing offshoots become more widespread within service organizations, it becomes imperative to build bridges between practices in order for design to rediscover its role in the making and as a value integrator that is crucial for survival considering the actual predominantly creative economy.

Truth is, one can spend a life blindly shouting that design needs to be taken seriously as a strategic asset within startups and modern organizations. But mountains start to move when we hit the road to develop a deeper understanding of how these organizations function and how they work to generate their offers, for that is the only path to end-to-end integration between design and strategy. And that is my goal with this book.

I'm a designer, and over the last decade I have founded two global service design agencies and an entrepreneurship acceleration program through design that took the shape of a service innovation school. On that journey, I've been involved in numerous projects aimed at helping Fortune

500 companies and startups align design with their strategy and production methodologies. From experience I can tell you that even though it's not simple, it can, and must, be done. My intention with this book is to approach this necessary integration not as a lean manufacturing specialist, which I am not, but as a designer that has faced and solved this puzzle many times.

THE DESIGN THINKING MYTH

Before we go any further, it will help if you have a glimpse into my mindset on the "Design Thinking" buzz movement.

The term Design Thinking has blurred origins and was pushed by several design consultancies, the most prominent of them being IDEO. It refers to how designers approach problems and their methods of problem solving.

Despite the premature announcements of its death by journalists, Design Thinking is growing. It recently gained steam inside Fortune 500 organizations and business consultancy companies like McKinsey and Accenture. Being involved in service design projects around the globe over the last decade has made clear to me that high-ranking professionals and C-level executives are now buying into it. There has been a growing hum of excitement around it, and many now want to be involved with projects that are design-based.

When people ask me what I think about all the buzz around the "Design Thinking" term, my answer is: I'm loving it. If buzzwords are what it takes to make leading organizations rethink the role of design within their operations, then I'll take it.

Design Thinking sparked a rescue movement for the original purpose of design, defined by the Bauhaus during the '20s, and it's helping push design back into business strategy, a place it never should have left.

However, as with any buzzword, there is a tendency for basic misconceptions to arise. Here are some common, and a bit irritating, affirmations you may find around the term:

"Design Thinking is a new form of design: It is design applied to business."

We really don't need any "new form of design." That kind of thought is a reflection of the industrial mindset that calls for specialization, the same one that supported the fragmentation of design into disciplines during the post-Bauhaus era. The true nature of design lies in the integration between humanities and the industry, and, as such, has always been business-sensitive.

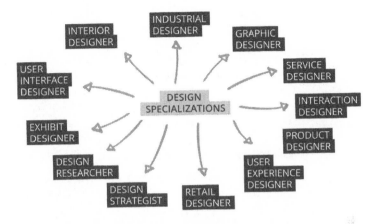

"Design Thinking is a methodology"

A methodology has inputs, outputs and controls. It also follows a course of execution. To state that design is a methodology is to reduce design to a mechanical and predictive form of problem-solving. Because design is focused on creating variation, a design methodology is the same as having no design.

"Design Thinking is a toolbox"

Honestly, I hate this one.

To state that design is a toolbox is in conflict with the word "design" itself. In its mother language (German), the word design is spelled "Gestaltung." "Gestalt" refers to an organized whole that is perceived as more than the sum of its parts.

In design, what we really do is steal tools. No really: that's what we do. We steal them, and then we mash things up and play around with them to create design lenses that better suit our challenges.

For example, ethnography is a technique that we borrow and adapt from anthropologists; behavioral observation techniques come from psychology; we take business tools from marketing and administration; and we take movement dynamics from physics and biology.

Steve Jobs, Picasso, and T.S. Eliot said, "Good artists copy. Great artists steal." I guess they were all great artists.

Designers feel free to move through the world's infinite scientific and humanities resources, without having to carry the strict disciplinary burden of specialists. They take what they need from other fields and adapt it to better suit their challenges.

Design Thinking is not a toolbox. Life is the designer's toolbox.

"Design Thinking is dead."

When people state that Design Thinking is over, got killed or is stuck in the past, they reveal that they misunderstand it. These people only see Design Thinking as one of the forms mentioned above, and are often the ones who never got their hands dirty with design. In reality, we are barely scratching the surface of what design can do to improve organizations and people's lives in the actual economy.

We are shifting from an industrial Era to a sharing economy, one in which people are opting out of ownership and choosing more collaborative consumption models. And design plays a major role in promoting and sustaining this transition. So it is far from being dead.

With that in mind, this book is not about telling you that design or Design Thinking is important. I don't need to tell you to be empathetic, collaborative and experimental. This has been said many times, and I don't think there is the need for any new book to repeat it.

This book is a practical guide that explores how startup entrepreneurs and business leaders, who hold no design degrees, can integrate service design into their development cycles in order to create sustainable, desirable and profitable new services.

In the first part, The Concept, I will explore the reasons why we need to move away from the "make and sell" industrial logic we've been exploiting over the last century. To take its place I propose a new service-oriented mindset that carries the idea of "learn, use and remember users' journeys." In this part of the book, we'll discuss the challenges our industrial society is facing and the forces driving the current service-oriented economy. We'll also look at how design can help new businesses make this shift.

In Part II, The Practice, I will take you on a journey through the **MVS—Minimum Valuable Service**—model. This model can integrate service design into the Lean Startup or any Agile development cycle. It adds the human values needed to foster service innovations within the Lean's scientific approach. In this part of the book, you will learn tools, methods and practices that will help you get your hands dirty with design.

I'm eager to know your achievements. Enjoy the read.

Tenny Pinheiro

tenny@theservicestartup.com

NOT IN 1908?

———

Chapter Two

"Any monkey can earn an MBA."

— Bruce Dickinson

Angel investor, entrepreneur, commercial pilot and
Iron Maiden's lead singer.

I have a confession to make: I have an MBA. To be fair, many years ago it seemed like a great idea. As a serial entrepreneur since the age of thirteen, I was always fascinated with the business world. So I thought, why not?

And that was the only thing I discovered. Why not?

The issue had nothing to do with the specific program I chose. Most business schools seem very similar, and I signed up for one of the finest. So what happened?

Well, nothing really... just business administration as usual.

The Master of Business Administration program was originally created to support the industrial era. With the coming of the industrial age, a new class of factory workers developed and, with it, the need to manage them. In the early days of the Industrial Revolution, there were few leaders capable of managing frantic, unregulated factory workplaces.

The first MBA program began in 1908 at Harvard University. The program was built to prepare leaders to better understand and navigate the new industrial age. It helped eliminate the heuristic use of best guesses and gut feelings in management, a common practice those days. Problem was, organizations were getting too complex. To thrive in the new economy, they needed to elevate their management capacity and have access to a well-prepared, yet expendable, workforce.

1908 was an iconic year for the industry for yet another reason. It was the year Henry Ford created what was about to become the most emblematic product of the modern era: the Model T, which he ingeniously merged with the new production assembly-line techniques.

In order to optimize production efficiency and reduce costs, Ford decided to make the Model T available in only one color: black. The reasoning behind it was quite simple: black paint dried faster, and that meant faster production. This opened the door for a new era of business decisions that would prioritize production efficiency over customer experience and satisfaction. Since educational models historically adjust their programs to fit existing market demands, the educational model followed suit.

Over the ensuing decades, with the rise of a more sophisticated consumer society, people became more demanding with the expectation of having many product choices. This marked the start of more modern production methodologies that ended up taking Fordism's place, enabling companies to offer more quality and variety from their production lines. Toyota initially paved this road by creating what they later called TPS, the Toyota Production System.

TPS was developed to get rid of what Toyota called "muri, mura and muda," which means "overburden, inconsistency and waste," respectively.

The belief was that production should operate without unnecessary stress, be capable of lowering variation, and repeating predictable results with minimum waste. The TPS method outlines seven forms of waste:

- Waste of over-production (largest waste).

- Waste of time on hand (waiting).

- Waste of transportation.

- Waste of processing itself.

- Waste of stock at hand.

- Waste of movement.

- Waste of making defective products.

The inspiration for the TPS came from supermarkets. Taichii Ohno, one of its creators, was fascinated about the way supermarket shelves functioned. In a supermarket, customers take what they need and the missing items are promptly restocked on the shelves. That observation was key to the implementation of the low inventory levels system. With it, parts were only replaced in the exact quantity needed to restock the inventory shelf—a very significant lean improvement brought to manufacturing by the TPS.

The later Lean Manufacturing methodology is a direct descendant of the TPS, and also the main inspiration for the creation of the Lean Startup approach.

Today, more than 100 years later, modern organizations and the corporate cultures that accompany them are still largely shaped by the logic that emerged from those smoky, industrial days. Frameworks for production and business decisions that were present then still persist today. This legacy shows itself in annoyingly odd rules and enforced old-fashioned attitudes that make no sense to anyone and are in deep collision route with the current younger generations.

The workstation myth, or "If you are not at your desk, you are not being productive."

Factory workers only perform at their workstations. There is where they find all the tools needed to carry out their jobs. This is where the despicable and irritating idea of "if you are not sitting in your cubicle, you are probably not working" comes from.

Departmentalization, or "It is not my problem, I will transfer you to another... "

Production lines are serialized. They work with inputs and outputs. The modern corporation was divided in the same way into small units of command-and-control called departments. Each department has its own agenda and needs to be able to receive inputs and produce outputs to other departments. Departments are conceptualized as manufacturing parts within a larger corporate factory machine.

Specialization, or "Not my fault... My role is only..."

It is far more efficient to replace small parts that perform specific functions than do it with larger and more complex parts. Larger parts could halt overall production if they need to be replaced. Dividing performance into small bits was a clever choice when dealing with machines. With humans, it worked much in the same way. An employee involved with every aspect of the business is difficult to manage, control and replace. On the other hand, an employee that understands and acts in only a specific part of the organization is expendable. The artisan holistically understood the entire development process, but the industrial worker was expected to specialize in a task or field of expertise. The demand for specialists was high during the Industrial Revolution and remains high today.

Human resources, or "Humans as resources."

In the factory, people were treated as an essential part of the machine. Human hands and limbs were needed in order to ignite production at the new smoke-breath monsters. As an appalling example, children were often employed in factories because they were small enough to fix the equipment from the inside.

Today we are not enslaving children as a business practice anymore. Well, maybe we are in some countries. But overall, this is seen as abusive. Nevertheless, many current HR department policies and "carrot and stick" practices still can be traced back to the industrial age.

While it is true that companies are starting to understand that there's more to human relations and welfare than training and benefits, most HR professionals still use terms like "human capital," "resources" or "head-count" when referring to employees.

The boring dress code, or "Why can't I wear my piercing?"

Suits were first introduced to the upper classes of society as a lighter clothing option during summer months. Over time, they moved into the workplace as a uniform. Have you ever thought about why people never wear white suits to work? During the industrial age, the blue- and white-collar workers could not keep the bright suits clean while wearing them in the factory environment. It just wasn't practical. White suits became a symbol of wealth and status, while black suits became the dress code of many organizations.

The list continues on. It is intriguing, the things we can learn about wicked practices that are still shaping the social status quo today, just by looking back to the industrial age.

Regarding education, throughout the last century business schools educated leaders to keep the smoke-and-mirrors of the industrial revolution alive. Their lectures on Administration and Marketing deserve their spot in modern business history. They were instrumental to the last century of business decisions and there are good practices that, still today, can be gleaned from those disciplines. However, today's business dynamics have gained new layers of complexity.

By taking a hard look at the traditional, "make and sell" industrial processes and education, and at our actual, "de-objectified" and relational service economy, one cannot help but to notice the obvious conflicts.

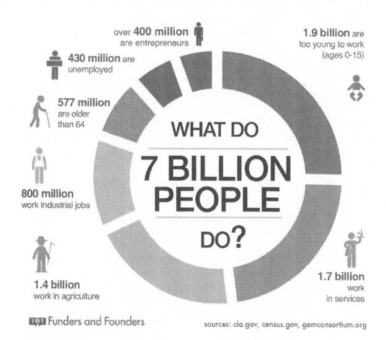

Fig: Above the info-graphic showing that the larger part of the active population work in services. (Source: http://notes.fundersandfounders.com/post/50947479488/what-do-7-billion-people-do)

Market exchanges are no longer just about production, transactions and a streamlined value chain anymore. To limit the term "business" within the boundaries of that simple logic is to ignore the real organic complexity of business organisms like Amazon.com, Airbnb.com or Apple's iTunes. Those entities are not suitable to be analyzed under the lens of traditional '60s Marketing tools. Their forward-thinking structures are leveraged by many new underlying dynamics; innovations like peer-to-peer value generation, overly distributed value networks and a mix of personalization and mass distribution (also called mass customization), to mention just a few.

A new business logic is drastically needed. One that allows us to shift our strategic lens from products (goods) to services, from transactions to relationships, and from ownership to access. One that empowers leaders to make decisions based not on streamlined and optimized value-chains, but on decentralized value-generation practices. That enables companies to generate value in outside-in mode, co-designing solutions with their customers in order to minimize the waste represented by the vast majority of poorly designed offers that we can see cluttering the market today.

For startups, this dilemma represents a critical path. In order for those under-dogs to innovate and survive, there's need for them to evolve to a more mature business logic, one that allows them to go beyond the focus on launching lean and fast, enabling them to also grasp for adherence, relevance and impact on their offers.

Photo: We definitely need a new logic.

I believe those small giants are the future. And as they are born with no legacy or binding pact with our smoky past, they have the opportunity to more easily instill the core of their business thinking with a more sustainable and humanized perspective.

Albert Einstein once famously said that we can't solve our problems by using the same kind of thinking we employed to create them. Perhaps he knew it's about time we shift to another logic in business.

WHAT IS A SERVICE?
A NEW LOGIC

———

Chapter Three

"…don't let anybody kid you. It's all personal, every bit of business. Every piece of shit every man has to eat every day of his life is personal. They call it business. OK. But it's personal as hell."

— Mario Puzo

The Godfather

Services are relationships, which makes them personal. When it comes to building long-term, meaningful relationships, Marketing and R&D approaches brutally fail. They really do on a grand scale.

The capacity to relate to one another is built in the human brain, and without it we would not be standing here today. This is true both for social and commercial relationships.

The human brain is wired to be relational. Michael Corleone was right, we can't help ourselves but to be personal all the time. Contrary to what many think, in our minds the lines are blurred between our personal lives and our business lives.

A similar blurring happens when a user engages with a service. However, in order to connect emotionally with their journeys, people have to first mentally humanize them, attaching to them personality traits and behaviors.

This explains why Harley Davidson conjures personalities and attitudes such as "grabbing life by the bars," and not numbers or product specifications such as "I'm riding a 800cc five-gear."

This mental process is called anthropomorphism, the attribution of human characteristics and behaviors to a thing or process. And this is a topic very dear to designers.

For designers, anthropomorphism is the doorway to interact emotionally with people. A designer's main goal within any project is to come out with something that creates seamless engagement and an emotional bond.

The well-designed service encourages people to go from the functional "Yup, it works," to the emotional "Wow, I love this and it says so much about me," or "This thing changed my life." Great designers excel at pushing the right anthropomorphic buttons.

At Livework, we refer to it as service envy. Service envy is the quest taken by our designers to create services that are more desirable than products. By creating service journeys that enable people to feel smart, safer and attractive, we believe the crave for ownership will gradually give space to the desire to access things whenever needed.

Access-based exchanges are already quickly overtaking ownership models in many economic sectors. There's no point in owning something without personal value, when in fact what one really needs is access to it. Due to changing lifestyle factors or environmental awareness, consumers are starting to consider the ownership of ordinary things as impractical, expensive and unsustainable. This presents a huge challenge for the "make and sell" strategist.

Meanwhile, Marketing's idea for fostering relationships and emotional connections is to continue pushing for mileage programs, SMS propaganda, TV ads and discount coupons.

The 2013 edition of the Nielsen Group report titled "Global Trust in Advertising and Brand Messages" showed "Recommendations from people I know" as the most important trust-building mechanism, according to responders. Now, as crazy as this may seem, this means people will trust a friend's opinion about your service, or even a stranger's opinion, before giving ears to what you have to say about it.

FORM OF ADVERTISING	TAKE ACTION	TRUST	DIFFERENCE ACTION VS. TRUST
Recommendations from people I know	84%	84%	--
Consumer opinions posted online	70%	68%	2%
Ads on TV	68%	62%	6%
Branded websites	67%	69%	-2%
Ads in newspapers	65%	61%	4%
Emails I signed up for	65%	56%	9%
Editorial content such as newspaper articles	64%	67%	-3%
Ads in magazines	62%	60%	2%
Brand sponsorships	60%	61%	-1%
TV program product placements	58%	55%	3%
Billboards and other outdoor advertising	57%	57%	--
Ads served in search engine results	57%	48%	9%

Interestingly enough, the research shows that traditional TV ads are still strong, but are now ranked third when you consider "take action" and "trust" as filters. Even so, this reality doesn't reflect how companies keep spending their resources, attempting to build trust.

Although business leaders today love to talk about relationships and the customer experience, there's not much backing up that talk. Post-transaction relationships are usually considered a sunk cost, a necessary evil to the "make and sell" organization. Their offerings are designed to be a "one-chunk" delivery, in which the company makes its money by pushing the transaction, not by creating relationships. With this model, it eats into profits to develop and maintain after-sales customer relationships.

Photo: Funny, right? But sadly, a reality for many service businesses nowadays. Source: Johnny Luzzini (whosay)

Even organizations that rely on long-term engagements, like banks or fitness centers, still can't find a better way to make profits than by pushing products and services to people when they don't even need them. Banks practically own their customers for life, and yet they are not relational enough to understand how to provide services that actually respond to people's real needs, desires and moments in life.

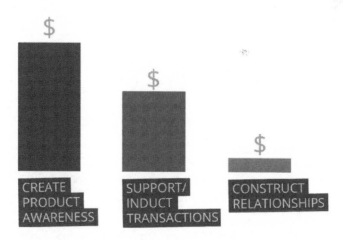

Fig: An x-ray of the budgeting strategy for the "make and sell" organization.

This mindset is what justifies decisions such as the outsourcing of contact centers or the adoption of low-wage policies to customer-facing staff. The "make and sell" logic gets in the way of delivering great service experiences.

Zappos.com have beat up that logic.

I've been to Zappos.com headquarters in Las Vegas and had the opportunity to deep-dive into their departments and shadow contact center employees while they answered customers' calls, and had a conversation with Tony Hsieh, Zappos founder and CEO. I have to say that I was immensely impressed to see how Zappos is rethinking traditional "make and sell" practices and succeeding big time in doing that.

The organizational DNA of Zappos is completely relational-based, from the way they self-identify as a service company to how they deal with their employees and customers on a daily basis.

This mindset is woven through the company's practices and can be seen everywhere, starting with their call center, or as they call it, Customer Loyalty Team. Instead of outsourcing this responsibility, like many companies do, Zappos made their call center a central part of the customer experience.

In order to properly do that, Zappos started from within, choosing a different path when it comes to shaping the workplace culture. Instead of marginalizing the contact center employees, the people who work on the Customer Loyalty Team are treated like rock stars. After all, they are the only ones, in an online retail operation, to actually have the opportunity to interact with the final consumer. They are the ones tasked with providing an awesome service, a service that reflects Zappos' entire organizational ethos.

And they do.

Interviewing a Customer Loyalty Team employee, I asked her if she enjoyed her work even when angry customers called with complaints. "That's when I love it the most," she responded, adding, "I love the challenge of turning them around in one call, and here I really have the toolset and space I need to do it."

The brand awareness, likability and perception of Zappos shot through the roof over the last years, propelled by great stories originating in the call center, and spread around the globe by social media and other outlets. A great illustration of the Zappos' culture is the pepperoni pizza story. The following is an excerpt from Tony Hsieh's book, *Delivering Happiness: A Path to Passion, Profits and Purpose.*

I'm reminded of a time when I was in Santa Monica, California, a few years ago at a Skechers sales conference. After a long night of bar-hopping, a small group of us headed up to someone's hotel room to order some food. My friend from Skechers tried to order a pepperoni pizza from the room-service menu, but was disappointed to learn that the hotel we were staying at did not deliver hot food after 11:00 p.m. We had missed the deadline by several hours.

In our inebriated state, a few of us cajoled her into calling Zappos to try to order a pizza. She took us up on our dare, turned on the speakerphone, and explained to the (very) patient Zappos rep that she was staying in a Santa Monica hotel and really craving a pepperoni pizza, that room service was no longer delivering hot food, and that she wanted to know if there was anything Zappos could do to help.

The Zappos rep was initially a bit confused by the request, but she quickly recovered and put us on hold. She returned two minutes later, listing the five closest places in the Santa Monica area that were still open and delivering pizzas at that time.

Now, truth be told, I was a little hesitant to include this story because I don't actually want everyone who reads this book to start calling Zappos and ordering pizza. But I just think it's a fun story to illustrate the power of not having scripts in your call center and empowering your employees to do what's right for your brand, no matter how unusual or bizarre the situation.

As for my friend from Skechers? After that phone call, she's now a customer for life.

Another great example of the commitment Zappos has to the establishment of long-term relationships with its customers is when an item is out of stock or not in the catalog. In that case, members of the Customer Loyalty Team find another store that carries the item and pass on this information to the customer. Though they may not be able to facilitate a transaction and close the sale, they can still provide a great service. Zappos employees know their primary job is to serve the customer, not the transaction.

Don't get me wrong, I'm not asking you to go Mother Teresa on your business strategy. Zappos grew from a $1.6 million profit to over $1 billion in less than 8 years. Its contact center Net Promoter Score, a well-known index used to measure customer advocacy, was 92% out of 100% the last time I checked, which is almost unheard of for a call center. For benchmarking purposes, Amazon.com NPS score is 76%.

Even though this makes a lot of sense, it is not like change is on the horizon for the "make and sell" organization. Most organizations are not like Zappos, and continue to operate under the perspective that services are like products, only intangible products.

The influential magazine *The Economist* defines service in its business glossary as "products of economic activity that you can't drop on your foot, ranging from hairdressing to websites."

Well, even though the decoder of my cable TV is an inseparable part of the cable provider service, it could easily, and painfully, be dropped on my foot.

Some organizations try to reduce this dissonance by packaging their services. This happens when a bank calls to offer a new "financial product" or when a travel agency offers you a "family package." These are all services being wrapped in a hollow product shell.

I wish I could tell you that the only issue here is the name given to those services, but truth is, this is just the tip of the iceberg. This "just put it in a box and sell it" attitude affects everything, from the way those services are designed to the way companies set up their organizational infrastructure to support the service delivery.

Sadly, the "make and sell" logic is all over the place. The classic marketing definition of services calls for "intangible products." But services are not products (goods), and are definitely not intangible. If that were the case, there would be no way to have access to them. Contrary to that, a service can be tracked and interacted with through the use of what service designers call "service evidences." Service evidences are avatars of a service that are there to make sure you can interact with the service, learning, using and remembering your experience. These are the three most important aspects of the service experience.

Learn

The process of learning about a service differs from products, since services are journeys. In order to learn about a product, such as an electronic gadget, one could read through the manual and fiddle around with it before first officially using it. This is made possible due to production methodologies that are employed to lessen variation and ensure consistency. That means a product is supposed to work in the same way every time you use it.

This is definitely not the case with services.

A service performance is the result of the collision between the user behavior, the execution plan (process), and the provider performance.

Considering that, services are co-produced journeys, woven by a constellation of interactions. That means the overall performance of a service depends on all actors and touch-points involved, which opens space for constant performance variations.

One cannot learn everything about a service performance by reading a manual. The only way to gain knowledge about a service is to engage and expose yourself to it.

Great services are usually easy to learn and master.

Use

Services are marketed as performance promises. This means, the value is only realized by the user when engaging with the service. A company can offer you an amazing Caribbean vacation, but the only way to truly evaluate their service is to pack your bags and fly to Cancún.

Also, service users intuitively know, and somehow expect, that consistency will fluctuate and be unpredictable between journeys.

So, contrary to products that behave consistently most of the time and can more easily seduce you via shelf presence or be validated through previous experiences, services are time-spans, journeys that need to be experienced in order to be truly evaluated.

Great services are accessible and seamless.

Remember

Service interactions can happen in a matter of seconds, and sometimes it can be difficult for somebody to even realize that anything occurred. A huge challenge for the design of services lies in leaving behind evidence that informs users that a service took place. One good example is the folding, tie-like, of hotel toilet paper left by the maid to signalize that the room was cleaned up, or chocolates left on the pillow. Those are all service evidences carefully designed to inform the user about a service performance. The focus of a service evidence is to generate knowledge as an output to the parts involved in the exchange.

Another crucial aspect related to the power of remembering was stated by Daniel Kahneman in his book *Thinking Fast and Slow*. In it, Daniel affirms that, in the end, it is the memory that matters, not the experience, per se. According to Kahneman's research, people have two selves—the experience self (the self that experiences things) and then the remembering self (the self that is made up of memories of those experiences).

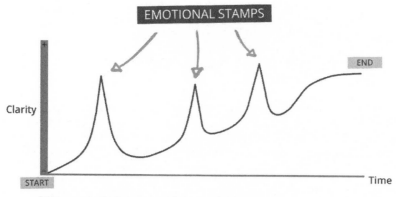

| Memory retrieving pattern for a service journey

The figure above is a representation of how people use to remember their service journeys. The experience itself is not the memory, what in Marketing literature people used to call "experience" is, in fact, the way people organize their memories regarding a set of already experienced interactions. This should not be mistaken by the cognitive touch itself; neither is it the intention that drives it. In the MVS Journey, presented in Part 2, I propose a clear separation between intention and interaction.

Emotional peaks created by moments where expectations were surpassed, or the user faced critical issues, play an important role on people's ability to clearly remember things. Still, a bad end is strong enough to contaminate people's entire image of the experienced service.

Good services are well-crystallized, making them easy to use and recognize. They also have the ability to translate into delightful memories.

It should have become clear at this point that services are of a completely different breed than products (goods), and thus the development approach to services should also consider different nuances. The Service Startup has the "learn, use and remember" journey imprinted in its soul. It holds a distinctly service-oriented core, dodging the inefficiency of the "make and sell" trap.

"It is wrong to imply that services are just like products 'except' for intangibility. By such logic, apples are like oranges except for their appleness."

With that argument in 1977, G. Lynn Shostack opened her famous article in the *Journal of Marketing*, entitled "Breaking Free From Product Marketing" (1977)*. Lynn, VP of Citibank at that time, wanted to prove that the product-centered mindset that had been fueling marketing decisions since the Industrial Revolution made for poor decision-making in the current service economy. She went further in asking: "Can financial services be marketed under the same premises that made Tide, the soap, a huge success?"

Shostack's idea of a market offer was not of the object and its package, but a complex molecular structure integrating tangible and intangible resources.

EXHIBIT 2
Scale of Market Entities

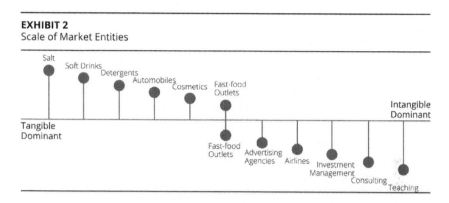

* In the infographic, Lynn is suggesting a variation between tangible and intangible dominance, according to different market entities.

Shostack's perspectives were later taken a step further by professors Stephen Vargo and Robert Lusch in their article entitled "Evolving to a New Dominant Logic in Marketing," published in 2004.

In the article, the two professors proposed a new logic for marketing that completely eliminated the idea of products (goods). For Vargo and Lusch there are no goods, only service, and what we call goods are simply objects representing parts of a service ecosystem.

According to the two professors, this service-centered view of marketing is also customer-centric. This means much more than simply being consumer-oriented; it means collaborating with and learning from customers by adapting to their needs. They also added that, in a service-oriented logic value is defined by and co-created with the consumer, rather than determined by the provider.

	Traditional Goods-Centered Dominant Logic	Emerging Service-Centered Dominant Logic
Primary unit of exchange	People exchange for goods. These goods serve primarily as operand resources.	People exchange to acquire the benefits of specialized competences (knowledge and skills) or services. knowledge and skills are operant resources.
Role of goods	Goods are operand resources and end products. Marketers take matter and change its from, place, time, and possession.	Goods are transmitters of operant resources (embedded knowledge); they are intermediate "products" that are used by other operant resources (customers) as appliances in value-creation processes.
Role of customer	The customer is the recipient of goods. Marketers do things to customers; they segment them, penetrate them, distribute to them, and promote to them. the customer is an operand resource.	The customer is a coproducer of service. Marketing is a process of doing things in interaction with the customer. The customer is primarily an operant resource, only functioning occasionally as an operand resource.
Determination and meaning of value	Value is determined by the producer. It is embedded in the operand resource (goods) and is defined in terms of "exchange-value."	Value is perceived and determined by the consumer on the basis of "value in use." Value results from the beneficial application of operant resources sometimes transmitted through operand resources. Firms can only make value propositions.
Firm-customer interaction	The customer is an operand resource. Customers are acted on to create transactions with resources.	The customer is primarily an operant resource. Customers are active participants in relational exchanges and coproduction.
Source of economic growth	Wealth is obtained from surplus tangible resources and goods. Wealth consists of owning, controlling, and producing operand resources.	Wealth is obtained through the application and exchange of specialized knowledge and skills. It represents the right to the future use of operant resources.

* Six differences between the goods and service-centered dominant logics. Vargo and Lusch (Evolving to a new Dominant Logic for marketing)

The impact of Vargo and Lusch's article was huge: it became the most-cited marketing article of the twenty-first century.

Maybe you're thinking, "that's really interesting, but what has this got to do with the Lean Startup movement?" Well, nothing, really. And that's exactly the point. This is the root of the problem this book is addressing.

As I've put it previously, the Lean Manufacturing approach was created to empower companies to thrive in a "make and sell" economy. This means the Lean Startup inherits its product-based, "make and sell" perspective. As such, it lacks crucial structures needed to equip a startup to navigate the current service economy.

In the following chapters I will explore the differences between the Lean Startup and the service design approach on a philosophical and practical basis, and, instead of just focusing on those differences, this book proposes a way to seamlessly integrate both approaches into the making.

FROM PRODUCTS TO SERVICES: AN INDUSTRIAL DILEMMA

As an industrial designer, I've been in the durable consumer goods industry for more than 30 years. I've been involved in hundreds of product projects that, without a doubt, have brought comfort and wellbeing to thousands of homes.

Throughout my career I saw that warm baths, refrigerated bedrooms, cold beers, and tasty meals are universally desired amenities. These are only made possible thanks to the work of engineers and designers who constantly push the limits of technology. Their work led us to more sustainable levels of water and electricity consumption in washing machines, refrigerators, and to smaller and more efficient microwaves.

In other industries, we see more efficient cars, TVs with increasingly better images, smartphones that connect us with everything...

However, my experience shows me that we have entered an industrial rat race, which means we keep competing against ourselves, product-by-product, feature-by-feature, in the pursuit of better and less expensive solutions.

On one hand, some products have become increasingly accessible to sections of the world population who, until now, could not enjoy their benefits. On the other, we are producing more and more stuff, multiplying products, occupying more and more space in our bags, kitchens, bedrooms, streets and avenues. And there is a limit to it.

A new era brings new challenges and, with it, new consumer behaviors. Several green behavioral trends and promises are beginning to translate into real initiatives. Years of sustainability speeches have brought great advances, but there is still a very long way to go.

However, what if instead of worrying so much about making more sustainable products, we shift the industrial logic to search for new consumption models that deliver the same benefits in a different way?

This implies a change in perspective that can help us better tackle the real problem.

Maybe what we need is not a car that stays parked for extended periods, but one that we can access whenever we need it, that opens space to transform the garage into a cool playground for the kids

Another good example of disruptive dematerialization lies in the entertainment industry. Over the last decade we have seen this industry shift media from VCRs to DVDs and then Blu-Ray, in a clear incremental effort toward better image quality. Now those pieces of plastic that used to sit on shelves are becoming obsolete, and slowly being replaced by on-demand streaming services.

In a future that isn't so far away, companies will no longer sell products, but exchange services.

Experiments are already taking place in a wide range of industries including the automotive. Big automobile brands are beginning to provide car-sharing services, where they sell access to their cars instead of ownership. We can see the rise of new consumption models like the pay-per-use or the rent-to-own models, an arrangement in which the user rents the product and can choose to keep it or return it at the end of the contracted period. Goods already entering these models range from tools, utensils in general, and even tires.

We have made a similar decision here at Whirlpool when it comes to our water purifier. The logic behind it is very simple. Unlike the rent-to-own model, we keep the ownership of the product focusing only on providing the service to the user. We are responsible for delivering a quality service—fresh and clean water in abundance—releasing the user from the responsibility of keeping the purifier clean, changing its filter and even discarding it at the end of its lifecycle.

Whirlpool has been working on improving this business model for over ten years now. We strongly believe the experience gathered from this will be key to keep a competitive edge in the future. And, most important, it grew to become a much more profitable model than the old "make and sell" version of it.

The bottom line here is that the companies that are ready to innovate over the next years are the ones who remain sensitive to the fact that there are an increasing number of users who prefer access to ownership.

This will require a fundamental change in the way companies craft their customer relations strategies, including the way they need to prepare their workforce to interact with customers that are informed, critical and aware of their rights and responsibilities.

The way objects are designed will also change, with designers being more concerned with finding solutions that can be better customized, have easy maintenance, constant update capability and built for extensive reutilization.

This revolution is bringing unprecedented change to the whole industrial value chain. Soon there will be no point for the user to keep spending large amounts of money in things that will, for the most time, only occupy space on shelves. This race has begun.

Mario S. Fioretti

**Industrial Design & Innovation Director
Whirlpool Latin America**

Photo: The shift from the "make and sell" approach to a service logic is not only necessary to foster innovation, it has become essential to ensure our society has a future.

PRODUCTS ARE AVATARS

Chapter Four

"The importance of physical products lies not so much in owning them as obtaining the services they render."

— Philip Kotler

1977

What most people call products I like to call service avatars.

Avatar is a funny word. For many what comes to mind when they hear it is the blockbuster movie directed by James Cameron. If that's true for you, then you actually already know everything you need to know about avatars.

The word avatar has Hindu origins. It means "a vessel on earth that represents an intangible entity."

When we shift our perspectives from products to services, we are not negating or ignoring the existence of objects, but refocusing from the object to its true purpose—its intangible entity—the service it conveys.

In my classes, I've been asked tons of questions about different objects and how they could possibly be services. The one I get most often is: "How about objects of art. How are they service avatars?"

A painting hanging on the wall can be a service to propagate one's tastes and way of thinking to others. Or it can be used for the purpose of giving life to an environment. These are all good and desirable services. When you feel that those objects of art no longer represent your tastes, or no longer suit the room, they will probably move out of service. They are then put into storage, sold, or donated.

Acquiring a service-oriented mindset includes the recognition that the objects that surround us are not products but service avatars. The object's service is the only thing that truly matters in the end. The service it provides is the real source of value.

The Service Startup can do that. This makes it lean, as there's no point in sustaining or developing interactions that serve no one. It also tends to be human-centered, as its founders have to be fully aware of their users, considering they are co-producers of the service.

This humanistic attitude constantly reminds the development team to stay away from the classic "technological feature creep" trap and keep them empathetically connected with its users' "learn, use, and remember" journeys.

Some may think that this attitude would come naturally, or that it's common sense. But, as we can see around us, common sense is not always common practice. And as I wrote before, the natural path for marketers has always been to support the "make and sell" approach.

This is made clear when you compare the consumer journey commonly adopted by service designers, and present in part 2 of this book, with the purchase funnel, widely used by marketing professionals. The simple act of using a tool such as the marketing purchase funnel can make you drift toward a "make and sell" mindset.

Here is why. The marketing purchase funnel was designed to document the consumer journey from awareness to purchase (transaction). And that's pretty much it.

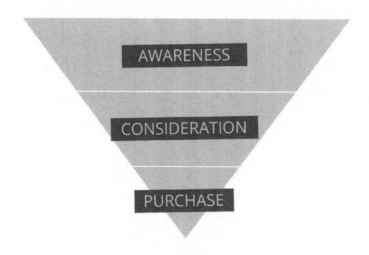

Fig: The Marketing Purchase Funnel.

Notice that the actual service performance, the delivery of the promise, doesn't even appear in the funnel.

This makes the purchase funnel an exclusionary and departmentalized "not my problem" tool. It's designed from a perspective that places marketing, user experience, and operations in different silos within the organizational chart.

This is a good example of a "make and sell" marketing tool. However, if you look closely you will find traces of the "make and sell" perspective in almost every marketing tool available, including business plan templates like the ones used to inspire the creation of the Business Model Canvas (BMC), a visual tool, created by Alex Osterwalder, that supports the generation of business plans. The second part of this book includes a discussion around the BMC and a way to integrate it with the **MVS model**.

Back to the funnel, Marketing professionals have positioned themselves as experts of the pre-transaction market arena. They craft the promise and take care of the awareness strategies, but leave the actual service journey to other departments, or in most cases, to chance.

Meanwhile, the customer continues to experience the service and the brand as a whole. No wonder most organizations can't live up to their promises.

If an air travel passenger finds it difficult to navigate through an airport and arrives late to the gate, the flight is delayed. A marketing manager could argue that it is the passenger's responsibility to organize themselves and better plan their journeys in the airport, but reality's a bit blurrier than that.

Airlines lose money when they are parked on the ground, and make their money airborne. Considering that, a late arrival is actually good for no one, representing a big loss for both the airline and the passenger.

By reviewing the airline check-in processes using "learn, use and remember" journeys, a project team could escape the flat "make and sell" approach and devise solutions that better balance the company's relation with its users.

Using the **MVS model** described in Part 2, I worked on a project for a global airline company to help them with their flight delay issues. As a result, the design team created a simple concept of an application and SMS service that, based on the location of the passenger in the airport, keeps them informed of the time it takes to reach their gate. The mobile app includes real-time estimates of immigration lines, security checks and other time sensitive information. The app is a simple solution, but one that appeals to the user's "learn, use and remember" journey, reducing emotional stress for travellers and saving the airline from delay suits and profit losses.

Photo/Fig: A prototype for an app that helps users better navigate airports.

This solution is beyond the scope of the purchase funnel, however it strikes a chord and connects to users, reducing the classic airport anxiety that comes with running late. This becomes a positive memory, differentiating the company from competition in the mind of the customer when it comes to future purchases.

Everybody gains from a relational approach like that. In a service economy, it is always everyone's problem.

WHY SERVICE DESIGN?

Chapter Five

"*A customer is the most important visitor on our premises. He is not dependent on us. We are dependent on him. He is not an interruption in our work. He is the purpose of it. He is not an outsider in our business. He is part of it. We are not doing him a favor by serving him. He is doing us a favor by giving us an opportunity to do so.*"

— Mahatma Gandhi

First, what is a "Service"? Have you thought about it?

The formal Marketing definition of a service describes it as:

"...an economic activity offered by one party to another, most commonly employing time-based performances to bring about desired results in recipients themselves, or in objects and other assets for which purchasers have responsibility".

As you can see, Marketing's idea of a service is wrapped in commercial purchases and economic facades. But this explanation really doesn't do justice to the dynamics and diversity of the word "service."

If you explore global examples of the word "service" you will discover that its present in all cultures, no matter how remote, and is the foundation of most religions. To be of service to one another is hardwired into us, a part of our core nature as humans. Service is a fundamental path to our true purposes in life.

In 2013, the La Follette School of Public Affairs published a study on altruism and happiness. Researchers used the results of a 1957 survey of 10,000 high school graduates. They found that people who said in their mid-30s that helping others in their work was important were apt to report being more satisfied with their lives nearly three decades later.

On a philosophical note, we can also observe that many of the major spiritual leaders in human history, including Mother Teresa, Gandhi, Jesus Christ and the Buddha, have preached the path to illumination through the act of serving others.

A more current definition of service also stands for the fact that a service provides the ability to extend one's capacity to act. Think about it for a minute.

That professional who gives you a haircut, would you be able to get that very same result just by yourself? That would be a hassle, right? That is a good example of one's capacity to act being extended by the use of services.

So, as we can see here, there's more to the word "service" than an economic transaction.

I like to think of a service as a favor, assistance that a person, or system, performs on the behalf of another. This favor, to take place in a sustainable manner, needs to be balanced with proper compensation, and by compensation I do not mean only financial compensation. However, a compensation mechanism is important since it is the main engine responsible for driving the sustainment of the service exchange. After all, no one would continue to do favors on behalf of another if they don't feel emotionally or economically compensated.

Below, you can find the service compensation matrix showing some of the reasons why people may exchange a service. I've built this matrix during a mentoring session in order to give the startup team a helpful cross-check on how balanced in compensation their interactions were. Feel free to use it and populate it with new values.

Photo/Fig: The service compensation matrix. A visualization of the main drivers behind a service engagement.

As made evident by the approach of this matrix, in contrast to process engineering and scientific methodologies, service design mixes the humanistic perspectives of design with service oriented logic to offer an emotional and human-centered form of crafting new services and improving existing ones. Because of its empathetic approach it helps teams burrow deeper in decoding people's needs and expectations, and has a proven record on helping project teams in successfully engaging users in co-design practices.

The ability to involve users early, as co-designers, in the development process is essential, as it increases the likelihood of generating valuable results.

But before I go any further, let me clarify something. When I use the term service design, the last thing I want to is advocate another design specialization. First, like I said before, we don't need another design silo. Second, it's a contradiction for any designer to insist on a narrowly-defined specialization. A service design project may require the use of interaction design, graphic design, product design, architecture and more. It would be crazy and shortsighted to place service design within a separate disciplinary structure, limiting it as an autistic practice.

Service design is a transdisciplinary practice. It is design in full swing, at the service of the current economy.

Also, the idea of "service" is too abstract to be defined as a distinct specialization. Applying design to services should not be a specialized practice nor an academic discipline, but recognized as an ability, skill and attitude that can be learned and applied by people with different professions, roles and expertise.

This should make clear that, from now on, whenever I use the term "service design," I'm referring to the practice and not to a specific profession, department or academic discipline.

In his book "What is a Designer," Norman Potter wrote that there are three kinds of design: the design of things; the design of places; and the design of messages. Early on, Potter was able to cut out all of the academic bullshit and give a focused explanation of design based on its practices, potential, and possible outcomes. However, he left a key practice out of his list. The design of "journeys". A journey is the main output of the service design practice.

All of this should not be confused with everyday knowledge. The artful design of complex service ecosystems does not comes easy and the service design practice have been maturing since it was created in 1991.

A little bit of background. service design was first introduced in Germany in 1991 by Dr. Michael Erlhoff as a design discipline at the Koln International School of Design (KISD).

In 2001, service design was introduced to the market, as a commercial practice, when Livework opened its studio in London. Livework was the first design agency dedicated entirely to the application of design to the development of services. Since then, a handful of agencies and organizations have been working to integrate service design into their customer experience practices around the globe.

Contrary to Experience Marketing, Customer Experience Management, or other similar business-case oriented disciplines, service design is a practice oriented for the make. What I mean by that is, it is well suited to empower a project team to orchestrate multi and cross-channel interactions aimed to deliver a solid user experience.

Parsons, The New School for Design, has been pushing the envelope on spreading the word about the service design practice.

Over the last two years I've been teaching a seminar for the school's MFA in Transdiciplinary Design. During the intensive, I guide the class in a deep-dive into a real project with a real client, where they experiment with every part of the service design practice firsthand. I believe learning by doing is the best (or maybe it is the only) way to acquire design skills. From problem discovery, to solution co-design, to the final presentation to the client, the students get fully exposed to service design tools and process.

Photo/Fig: Debrief session with Parson's students at a client facility in a project for a cancer treatment center in NYC.

Like any other design practice, service design encompasses a series of skills and competences that need to be toyed around with in order to become natural skills. It is known that the Industrial Design practice calls for a deeper understanding of production practices, materials and structures. Service design follows a similar logic; in order to orchestrate service ecosystems, you have to sink your teeth into its best practices, methods and proven tools.

The MVS model presented in the second part of this book will cast a light on this path and help you integrate service design into your startup's current development agenda.

"The successful development of a new service - a molecular collection of intangibles - is so difficult it makes new-product development look like child's play."

- Lynn Shostack - Breaking Free From Product Marketing (1977)

To design a service is to design a journey, and this means, ultimately, the design of moments in life.

When a user accesses a service, whether or not they pay for it, they are sharing the most important personal asset they have: their time.

The project team needs to be aware of this fact. Service designers are able to balance a full range of humanistic and performance variables in such a way that enables a service experience that is both seamless for the user and brings good business results.

The service design practice differs from the R&D product development approach by taking the perspective of the service users and actors in the ecosystem and then using that perspective to drive the design process.

In 2009, Airbnb.com was about to go bankrupt. The company had near-zero revenues and its founders were forced to max out their credit cards in order to maintain their operations. At that time, Airbnb was still part of the Y Combinator seed acceleration program, and its founders went on a mission to find what was going wrong with their concept.

It is common for early-stage startups running on small margins to be preoccupied with scalable actions and tech solutions with growth potential. But the Airbnb team, lead by co-founder Joe Gebbia, decided to try something else.

While browsing through their NYC listings, the project team noticed a troubling pattern: bad listing pictures. People were taking grainy photos using their phones, or using old pictures. It wasn't surprising, then, that they were not successful. Consumers couldn't even see what they might be paying for.

Following the advice of Paul Graham, the co-founder and mastermind behind Y Combinator, the team decided to grab some cameras, fly to New York, and take beautiful, clear, high-resolution photos of the listings.

After they uploaded the new pictures to the website, their weekly revenue doubled. This was the first financial improvement the company had seen in over eight months. Even more exciting, it was an excellent proof that they were onto something with their community website for rent-out lodging.

This is another great example of a hidden "learn, use and remember" issue, one that could mislead the team into thinking their solution isn't good enough for the market and needs to be changed, or pivoted, into something else. Luckily Airbnb didn't pivot their business and instead solved their issue with an early-stage prototype, one that became a service in itself. Today anyone with a listing can apply for professional photography at Airbnb.com, and it's free.

The Service Startup is fluent in service design. This means it takes an outside-in approach to the design of services, an approach that empowers the team to co-design solutions with users, and anticipate "learn, use and remember" issues by making use of early stage prototypes. I will discuss the How-Tos on co-design and early stage prototyping later in this book.

THE EISE MATRIX

Nothing is more disruptive than a service that combines high levels of uniqueness (differentiation) and human connection (relevance).

I=U+HC
Innovation = Uniqueness + Human connection

*In order to crystallize this thinking into the **MVS** model, I've created the Eise Matrix. The Eise matrix is a simple visualization tool designed to help startup founders with their launch and positioning strategies.*

*The matrix is based in the **I=U+HC** principle, and proposes four quadrants named: decay, sociopath, darling and prodigy.*

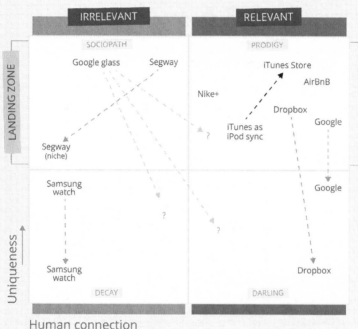

Landing Zone
Every startup naturally aims high on uniqueness, as there is no other way to fight old corporate dinosaurs when your company is that small.
The landing zone marks the most desirable zone in this chart for small players.

Gravity
The natural tendency is for losing differentiation steam as new players enter the market or the wow factor gets colder.

Reverse Gravity (pivoting)
In order to reverse gravity there's a need to rethink the underlying premises of the business.

As you can see in the matrix, the MVS model acts as a force pushing solutions up in the Human Connection axis. The Eise Matrix is available on the supporting materials workbook and it has the power to explain in simple visual terms the main reasons and consequences of adopting design into the business development process.

THE MIRROR OF VISIBILITY

Chapter Six

"It is not the strongest of the species that survives, not the most intelligent, but the one most responsive to change."

— Leon C. Megginson (yep, not Charles Darwin)

"Line of visibility" is a post-industrial concept that states that a service performance relies on, and takes place in, two different spaces: the front stage and the backstage.

The terms front stage and backstage are inspired by the structure of a theater performance. In theater, behind all the action happening on stage and visible to the audience, there are invisible performances carried out by a stage crew taking place off-stage. These behind-the-scenes actions are fundamental and vital parts of the play, even though they normally remain hidden to the spectators.

The idea behind this concept is that the line of visibility foregrounds the interactions experienced by the user and hides the chain of actions that support the service performance.

Even though the term "line of visibility" is ubiquitous in service management literature, the word visibility is poorly used here since it is not only to a person's vision that a service interaction appeals to, but all five human cognitive channels. The smell of fresh-baked cookies in a bakery may not be visible, but it is an appreciated user interaction.

The line of visibility concept reinforces the use of poor "make and sell" strategies that are not suited for the present-day economy. In order to better understand this affirmation, let's revisit the factory and its workforce distribution strategy.

Back in the old days in a manufacturing facility, the lower-level employees were the ones that manned the assembly and production lines. These were the low-wage workers of the Industrial Era, who had no say in the direction of the business, nor any sense of contribution or clear perception of growth. Assembly line workers were simply considered part of the manufacturing machine, an approach that back then worked well, as it was easier to mistreat and ignore employees that were invisible and had no role in delivering the customer experience.

Now, when we shift our lens to accommodate a service economy, the buffer between production and delivery is reduced to an almost nonexistent margin. Services are co-produced in the same moment as they are delivered, and today, there is not always a visual barrier between supporting and customer-facing interactions.

In a service economy the company culture jumps the counter. This means everything needs to be thought as if it is front stage, everything is part of the show. Take Disney as an example. Disney keeps alive the same amount of magic for its employees that it does for its customers. I've been through Disney's backstage and secretive tunnels, and it is revealing to see the amount of effort Imagineers, Disney's design team, put in creating touch-points and processes that are designed to delivery the magic also to Disney's employees. As they would have put it: "We need to protect the magic." Disney lives and breathes the fact that an employee, or "cast member" as they call it, is also a guest. This attitude is crucial to protect Walt's legacy.

There are numerous customer-facing interactions Disney extends to its employees; take for example the employees' pin trade exchange booths located in the tunnels or the fact that Mickey can't be seen walking backstage without wearing full costume.

Considering this paradigm shift, it is almost impossible to accurately trace Disney's line of visibility. After all, where is the backstage when there are onstage interactions happening behind the scenes?

This idea alone should encourage companies to rethink their service structures. Most often, though, they stick with what they already know. Modern organizations remain factory-like, only with glass windows and counters instead of big brick walls separating production from the customers.

A customer now essentially interacts directly with the production line, served by the modern-day version of the low-purpose factory worker. A company may spend millions of dollars on a Super Bowl ad, and designate its most disconnected employees to deliver its promises and represent its brand. Maybe you are thinking that this is illogical, but in fact it is just old logic.

Over the years I've collected numerous stories from customer-facing employees to C-level executives, in almost every sector of the economy across three different continents. No matter the location or industry, this troubling reality remained the same. I became accustomed to the nauseating feeling that would wash over me when bank account managers or retail employees would tell me that they've never stepped inside their company headquarters, have never met any C-level executives, and have never even been able to enjoy the same perks that their white collar office peers have access to.

The modern "make and sell" organization flipped the industrial hierarchical structure, exposing its bottom, turning the production-line employee into its customer-facing staff. Other than doing that, it didn't do much for the disconnection between the bottom and the top of the pyramid, sustaining the idea of keeping white collars and production workers worlds apart.

I call the application of this old industrial workforce logic to the current service economy the Mirror of Visibility.

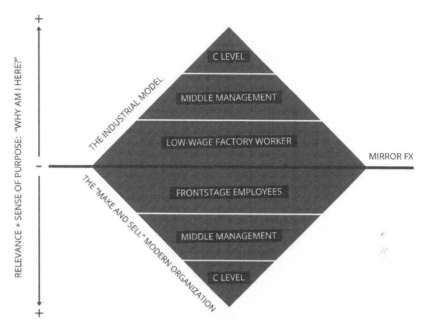

Photo/Fig: The mirror of visibility.

The Mirror of Visibility is yet another proof that the industrial "make and sell" approach that have dominated the 20th century is still alive and kicking in business structures today.

However, even though executives may think so, it is not the only, neither the most profitable, logic available. Zappos and Disney are proof that great results may come from abandoning the Mirror of Visibility.

And, before you may think so, this has no relation whatsoever to raising costs. If it seems costly to raise value and purpose for employees, the business model is wrong. A company's business growth should never be inversely proportional to building the sense of belonging and purpose of its employees.

The time when organizations would shackle workers to their stations has passed. In the current economy, everyone is exposed. Companies trying to operate with the mirror of visibility model blind themselves to opportunities. They will find innovation difficult and seldom provide great service experiences for their customers.

When a business leader believes profits can only be made on the backs of poorly prepared, easily replaceable, and unmotivated onstage workers, his business thinking has gone awry. These are poor "make and sell" instincts, ill-suited for the present-day economy.

The idea of what is expensive and what is profitable needs to incorporate a broader perspective. It's not unusual to see organizations downsize their workforce as a strategy to minimize costs. At the same time, such organizations waste millions of dollars in change requests and fixes due to bad project management. Companies outsource contact centers to save money, then spend more on advertising in order to fix the service issues this decision creates.

Now, that, right there, is highly illogical, as Spock would have put it.

And the bigger the organization grows, the more ingrained this crazy logic becomes in the business culture. That is why it is so important for startups to grasp a service-oriented mindset while they are still young, fit and agile.

For large organizations the mirror of visibility is, above all, a cultural puzzle. This jigsaw will never be solved only by the re-design of customer interactions. That would be the same as trying to kill cancer by treating only its symptoms. No. It requires digging into the company culture, revising its Taylorist baggage and re-thinking its business premises.

According to the interesting perspective of former MIT professor Edgar Schein, the underlying model for the corporate culture is composed by three main drivers: Assumptions, values and artifacts.

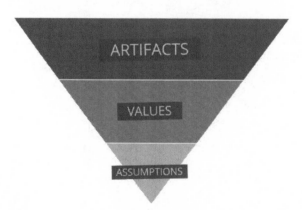

Assumptions - Deeply embedded, taken-for-granted behaviors that are usually unconscious but constitute the essence of the culture.

Values - Organization's stated values and rules of behavior. It is how the members represent the organization both to themselves and to others. This is often expressed in official philosophies and public statements of identity.

Artifacts - Include any tangible, overt or verbally identifiable elements in an organization. Architecture, furniture, dress code, and office jokes are good examples of organizational artifacts.

In order to impact the overall behavior of an organization, there is the need to design for each one of these drivers. This is not the main topic of this book, however, if you are interested in learning more about the implementation of a design core into a large organizational ecosystem, please refer to my article at Core77 entitled "Meta-service design, designing a way for design to survive in a toxic organizational environment." You will find a direct link to it in the references section.

Considering the discussed functional and ethical implications brought by the line of visibility, I have chosen to eliminate it from all the service representations in the **MVS model**. I will discuss those dynamics later in Part 2 of this book.

Peter Drucker was on the mark when he said, "culture eats strategy for breakfast."

FROM PROCESSES
TO JOURNEYS

Chapter Seven

"It is good to have an end to journey toward; but it is the journey that matters, in the end."

— Ernest Hemingway

The idea that our lives can be understood as journeys is not new, it's a concept that goes back to Joseph Campbell's hero's journey.

The hero's journey or, the mono-myth, is a basic pattern found in many narratives from around the world. According to Campbell, it represents the fundamental way we construct and tell our stories, and how we envision ourselves participating and living in them.

~JAMES CAMERON'S~

~Disney's~

~Pocahontas~ AVATAR.

In ~1607~ [2154] a ship carrying ~John Smith~ [Jake Sully] arrives in the lush "new world" of ~North America~ [PANDORA]. The settlers are mining for ~gold~ [unobtanium] under supervision of ~Governor Ratcliffe~ [Colonel Quaritch Jake silly]. ~John Smith~ [Jake] begins exploring the new territory, and encounters ~Pocahontas~ [Neytiri]. Initially she is distrustful of him, but a message from ~Grandmother Willow~ [the Tree of Souls] helps her overcome her trepidation. The two begin spending time together, ~Pocahontas~ [Neytiri] helps ~John~ [Jake] understand that all life is valuable, and how all nature is a connected circle of life. Furthermore she teaches him how to hunt, ~grow crops~ [tame dragons], and of her culture. We find that her father is Chief ~Powhatan~ [Eytucan], and that she is set to be married to ~Kocoum~ [Tsu'Tey], a great warrior, but a serious man, whom ~Pocahontas~ [Neytiri] does not desire. Over time, ~John~ [Jake] and ~Pocahontas~ [Neytiri] find they have a love for each other. Back at the settlement, the men, who believe the natives are savages, plan to attack the natives for their ~gold~ [unobtanium]. ~Kocoum~ [Tsu'Tey] tries to kill ~John~ [Jake] out of jealousy, but he is later killed by the settlers. As the settlers prepare to attack, ~John~ [Jake] is blamed by the ~Indians~ [Na'vi], and is sentenced to death. Just before they kill him, the settlers arrive. Chief ~Powhatan~ [Eytucan] is ~nearly killed~ [shot with arrows. yo], and ~John~ [Jake] sustains injuries from ~Governor Ratcliffe~ [Colonel Quaritch], who is then ~brought to justice~. ~Pocahontas~ [Neytiri] risks her life to save ~John~ [Jake]. ~John~ [Jake] and ~Pocahontas~ [Neytiri] finally have each other, and the two cultures resolve their differences. IMHO ~ MATT BATEMAN

Photo: Hollywood loves to use the mono-myth pattern to tell stories.

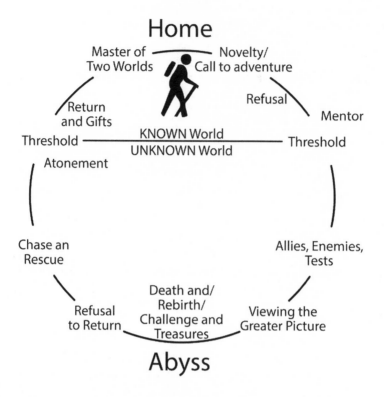

Home

Master of Two Worlds ——— Novelty/ Call to adventure

Refusal

Return and Gifts

Mentor

Threshold ——— KNOWN World / UNKNOWN World ——— Threshold

Atonement

Chase an Rescue

Allies, Enemies, Tests

Refusal to Return

Death and/ Rebirth/ Challenge and Treasures

Viewing the Greater Picture

Abyss

Photo/Fig: A classic representation of the hero's journey.

According to Campbell, in our minds, life is a journey divided by iconic moments where we see ourselves as heroes facing a quest.

As I wrote before, the design of services is also the design of journeys. Taking that in consideration, a project team needs to be able to shift their thinking from processes chains to user journeys. A perspective around journeys improves the team's levels of empathy and reveals contextual opportunities that are often missed by a transactional perspective.

This shift demands the ability to wear the users' shoes, and walk through the user's situation to uncover "learn, use and remember" issues and opportunities across the whole territory of exploration.

Other than by luck, one cannot design a valuable service without nurturing a good level of empathy for its users, while also developing an overall understanding of how, in their minds, they are living their journeys.

Σprocesses != journey

The sum of all processes does not equal the user journey.

Photo/Fig: A flight attendant's processes guidebook. Can you imagine the pilot's guidebook? Yet, most flight attendants are not fully aware of their users' journey.

Not long ago I oversaw a usability study for a large gas station chain in Brazil with the objective of mapping service issues perceived by users that were not covered by the company's internal process maps.

In Brazil, the auto-service on fuel pumps is prohibited by a union movement that claims new machines take away jobs and so the only way to have your tank filled is to wait to be served by "pump guys".

One thing that the team noticed while performing ethnographic studies at gas stations was that many bikers refused to dismount their motorcycles in order to have their gas pumped into the tank, while others would dismount but do so angrily. Some were even so offended by the request to dismount that they would drive off without getting their tanks filled.

The dismounting requirement is pretty simple. It's a regulation created in Brazil meant to protect the safety of the biker if something goes wrong.

So what was going on in the user's minds to induce them to behave so weirdly about a safety procedure?

The problem was that the bikers had no idea it was a standard safety regulation. They had a different perception of the reasoning behind it.

As we dug deeper into our investigation and interviewed bikers about the issue, we found something surprising. Not only were most of them unaware that this was a safety precaution measure, they thought the request to un-mount was to prevent them from driving off with full tanks without paying.

Photo/fig: Livework's design team immersed, working as pump attendants in order to uncover insights.

This combination of miscommunication and misunderstood perceptions shows how the sum of all processes never equals the user journey. While a journey is a connected, meaningful story within users minds, for the "make and sell" organization it remains a fragmented sum of transactional processes informed by the marketing purchase funnel.

I can guarantee that no matter how brilliant a project team's final design for the gas station may be, you cannot please customers that believe they are being treated like thieves. It's a psychological barrier that's almost impossible to break, one that would have been missed had users not been involved early on in co-designing sessions along with the project team.

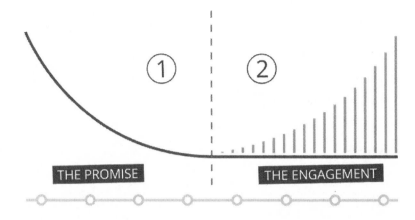

Photo/fig: The mirage effect. The journey is not a set of transactions, but a memory.

This infographic shows the journey the consumer takes to internalize and validate the promise against their belief systems (1). After the user chooses to engage with the service, a mental reframing process kicks in. This shifts and tweaks the meaning of the experience to better accommodate and align with the user's current mental models, which are the way a person perceives and relates to the world (2). The user journey is a direct result of this mental processing and, as such, it cannot be fully mapped with quantitative measurement tools.

This disconnect between straightforward process maps and real-world user journeys explains why it's so common to see engineering teams reporting positive results on key performance indicators, while the user is frustrated with irritating and out of touch services. This mirage effect results in a lot of spent capital and waste, as resources are directed to service improvements in areas that may not actually be the source of frustration for users. In the end, the user gets the impression that nothing is being done.

This lack of understanding around how users "learn, use and remember" their journeys can result in a bad service offer, full of usability issues that may sink a startup or, as a matter of fact, any business.

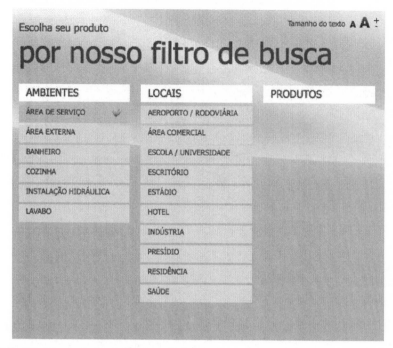

Photo/fig: The sink manufacturer's website navigation menu.

In the photo above the sink manufacturer company had the ridiculous requirement that the customer first needed to choose what kind of establishment they would be installing the sink in, before ever showing the user any sink models. The options ranged from prisons and stadiums, to hotels and airports. Not only was this extra interaction wildly unnecessary, but it forced the user to jump back and forth, revisiting each category just to make sure they weren't leaving some options out. While this architecture may reflect the organizational chart and processes of the manufacturer, it is far from reflecting the way people shop for sinks.

At the 2011 Service Design Network Conference in San Francisco, I made "from processes to journeys" the theme for my keynote speech. The model presented in Part 2 of this book was also inspired by the discussions that resulted from that talk. It also highlights the close relation between Joseph Campbell's mono-myth and my own experiences mapping and crafting user journeys.

THE LEAN STARTUP PROCESS FOR THE NON-ADEPT

"…progress of civilization has brought along with it much beclouding of realities and grave danger. Apparent economies may easily deceive us. But technical progress should never be the goal, only the means."

— Lazlo Moholy-Nagy

Maybe you are familiar with the Lean Startup concepts, or maybe you are hearing about it for the first time in my book. Either way, my intention here is to give you just enough information about it to get you started on the MVS model described in Part 2. Keep in mind you don't necessarily need to be a Lean Startup practitioner or even have read the book by Eric Ries in order to start working on the MVS model. That being said, Eric's book is a popular source of information about the development dynamics of startups.

The Lean Startup is a scientific-based methodology created by Eric Ries, inspired by a mixture of the scientific approach to production found in Lean Manufacturing and the principles of rapid development found in the Agile approach.

According to Eric's book, the "fundamental activity of a startup is to turn ideas into products, measure how customers respond, and then learn whether to pivot or persevere." Still, according to Eric, all successful startup processes should be geared to accelerate that feedback loop.

The result is a product development approach that keeps the focus of the startup on developing small incremental prototypes, instead of spending energy and incurring in the risks of deploying big chunk solutions to the market.

The Lean Startup methodology encompasses three stages: Build, Measure and Learn. Those stages are there for the team to understand they need to build quickly, measure the achieved results as soon as possible, and learn everything they can in the process.

Photo/Fig: The Lean Startup build-measure-learn feedback loop.

I have a lot of respect for Eric's work with The Lean Startup model, and applaud the impact he's had in the business world. It was clever, proposing the merge of a scientific production approach with the Agile loops of rapid development. Everyone involved in the startup ecosystem benefits from a business ideology that preaches a way to deliver solutions under low-resource conditions.

Steve Blank, a professor, author and serial entrepreneur also known for having inspired Eric in igniting the Lean Startup movement, wrote in his book, *The Startup Owners Manual*, that twentieth-century models of product development will not be able to do the work in the current economy.

Steve is correct. The scientific R&D frameworks that fueled the technological marathon towards innovation in the '60s, '70s and '80s can't guarantee business success in today's complex and volatile market landscape.

Nevertheless, the answer to this problem lies not in yet another standalone scientific approach.

Toyota experimented with this scientific disconnect the hard way and paid an expensive price for turning its TPS methodology into an organizational cult.

Recently, between 2007 and 2011, Toyota's brand started to lose equity after numerous incidents caused by sudden car acceleration, resulting in dozens of deaths and millions of units being recalled.

The Japanese business culture is grounded on what they call "tatemae" (what you are supposed to feel or do) and "honne" (what you actually feel or do).

The recent downfall of Toyota's brand is vastly attributed to its employees' decision to abandon intuition and creative thinking (honne) in order to devote blind obedience (tatemae) to TPS controls and measurement practices.

Considering that and other similar stories, it seems counterintuitive, to say the least, to advise startups to rely only on scientific approaches to innovation.

Huge organizations famous for having invested billions of dollars in scientific R&D methodologies over the last decades are now turning to design as a way to reconnect with their consumers and employees. Service design is being adopted as part of the core strategy in companies like Virgin Mobile, Mayo Clinic, Johnson & Johnson, Fidelity Investments and others, in order to connect their scientific practices with people's real-world experiences.

The Lean Startup movement raised genuine questions about the need for startups to launch fast and lean. That, in my opinion, is its ultimate remarkable contribution. However, it's high time that we move away from depending solely on its scientific "make and sell" inclination. Instead, we need to open the space to also draw from design's humanistic approaches. This will help install a human-centric core in the daily development practices of startups and, eventually, large organizations that are practicing Agile development approaches.

WHY LEAN STARTUP?

———

Chapter Nine

"You must be shapeless, formless, like water. When you pour water in a cup, it becomes the cup. When you pour water in a bottle, it becomes the bottle. When you pour water in a teapot, it becomes the teapot. Water can drip and it can crash. Be water, my friend."

— Bruce Lee

When I founded EISE, The School For Service Innovation, I entered the startup's game by becoming a mentor for dozens of startups, a jurist on many global startup competitions, and an angel investor.

But my routine was not always like that.

As the CEO for Livework in Brazil, my main focus was on helping Fortune 500 companies innovate their services in order for them to succeed in the actual economy. This reality is a bit distant from the rapid, lightweight and ephemeral startup universe.

Luckily the school, which runs an entrepreneurship acceleration through design program, gave me exposure and access to those underdogs of the business world. As a result, I became simultaneously obsessed with their universe and puzzled by their product-centered inclination and inability to use design as a part of their development routines.

Eise's five Drives:

1. There is only service. Products are service avatars.

2. All value is created over use, not ownership.

3. Innovation is a perceived value and, as such, cannot be imposed by the provider.

4. A service-oriented thinking is naturally more sustainable and human-centered.

5. To be of good service is directly connected to the pursuit of happiness and purpose in life. That can be found in most creeds and religions around the globe.

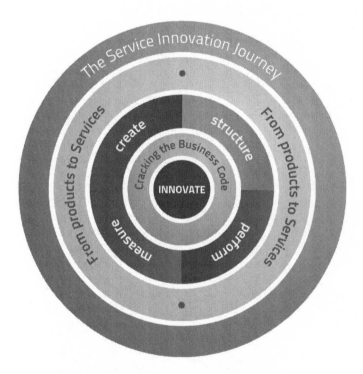

Photo/Fig: Eise's educational program: The Service Innovation Journey.

Lately I came to the conclusion that the reasons behind the lack of design in most startups come from a mix of two different things.

First, there is an overconfidence in their ability to tackle social problems using a code-driven approach. Literally most founders think they can code their way into their users' lives.

Secondly, the way design consultancies engage with clients, based on per project contracts, is not adequate, and only keeps design out of reach to startups. Plus, they are damn expensive. Today, even though there is an ongoing democratization of Industrial Design—which often goes by the names Design for all or Design within reach—the application of design to business strategy in commercial projects remains something upscale and vastly oriented to Fortune 500 companies.

This book took me two years of research, discussions, and hundreds of hours prototyping frameworks at different startup business scenarios. In my research I discovered some attempts to unite Lean Startup and Design Thinking, which included founders' initiatives, workshops and even some publications from dear friends of mine. However, they all operate at the level of tools, which isn't sufficient.

Lean Startup has a scientific core. Design has a humanistic core. These crucial differences in mindset and conceptualization need to be addressed in order for any combination of the two to work.

Properly integrating them requires finding the cultural link between those two worlds, with the resulting tools not becoming crazy mash-ups of existing tools, but a new fresh lens, borne from the harmonization of these two approaches to innovation.

Service Design	Lean Startup
Service Design is service-oriented.	Lean is product-oriented.
Design searches for solutions throughout a holistic approach, mixing practices and fields.	Lean is based on scientific thinking, and as such it preaches the pursuit of a solution through specialization and division (cohorts), analysis and tests.
Design is outside-in and co-participative, and involves the end-user in the early stages of conception.	Lean is inside-out and it involves the creation of an hypothesis first, then the involvement of users in testing and validation procedures.
Design welcomes variation and believes that in variation lies the source of potential innovations.	Lean is about reducing variation in production and believes that this reduction helps to better predict what you will get out of the resources you are committing to the process.
Design is empathy-driven. All value created is rooted in the deep understanding of how people live, work and relate to others. The ability to deep dive in the user's world and get valuable insights out of it is an intuitive ability of designers.	The TPS, Lean's precursor, has Genchi Gembutsu, a philosophy that preaches that a problem to be solved needs to be understood where it takes place. This philosophy inspired the phrase often used by startups: "get out of the building". Even though Genchi calls for some empathy, it is still a troubleshooting approach, not a pre-design empathy building practice.
An organization, product, or service can't create or deliver value. It can only propose value, since value is cognitively created in the user's mind. This is the basis of the belief that service journeys are always co-created between the provider and the user.	Value is created and delivered by the organization. "The critical first question for any lean transformation is: which activities create value and which are a form of waste?" "The value hypothesis tests whether a product or service really delivers value to customers once they are using it." Ries, Eric (2011-09-13). The Lean Startup: How Today's Entrepreneurs Use Continuous Innovation to Create Radically Successful Businesses

The list of deep conceptual conflicts is huge, which raises a red flag. You can't just get a tool from one approach and mix it with a canvas from the other when, fundamentally, both endure so many philosophical differences.

As I said before, I like Eric's approach. It's smart, execution-oriented and helpful. Not only that, it's really making a difference for the businesses of startup founders, venture capitalists, angel investors and, unexpectedly, big organizations that are aspiring to get lean and agile.

I believe that the Lean Startup, or any other Agile approach, if properly combined with design, can be a great asset for the development of innovative services. Agile approaches are fast-paced and iterative, forcing the project team to focus on getting quickly to a solution, instead of continuing wandering around infinite possibilities. For startups, resource management is a huge dilemma and one that has sunk many great business ideas around the globe.

Surprisingly, in his book Eric Ries mentions Design Thinking, but first he confuses it with a product development idea. In another instance, he places it in the context of an ideation technique and later on he mentions it along Six Sigma as a business and engineering philosophy, one that is focused on creating customer experiences.

As we should be able to tell, Eric has some stark misunderstandings about design, its origins, and underlying purpose. Yet Eric was right about one thing: the limitations around how actual design agencies engage with clients.

And as I've put it before, I agree with Eric on this one. The traditional design consultancy engagement model is doomed, and brings a lot of noise and static to the value creation process. One of the more disturbing issues is the constant interruption of the knowledge-building flow when consultancies jump in and out of an organization.

This alone is a huge obstacle to the learning process required to fostering innovation in startups (or any organization). To have the second increment round of a new service implementation performed by a different team than the one that conceived the first round hurts the organization's ability to learn and, along with it, its capability to innovate.

The ability to sustain the knowledge flow, characteristic of the Lean Startup iterative approach, is definitely an asset for businesses in the pursuit of innovations.

But design shall not be mistaken for the same as a design agency and I don't believe that the best approach to generating social and economical value should be through the development of hypotheses behind closed doors and then tests with users.

This idea is based on old scientific R&D models, and is insufficient for creating breakthrough innovations. Engineers and scientists have experienced first-hand that, when facing complex social and economical challenges, the shortest path between two dots is seldom the seemingly-obvious straight line.

Creativity is the answer for many of the economic and social issues we face, and the straightforward scientific approach is not known for its ability to unleash creative problem-solving.

"Efficiency programs such as Six Sigma are designed to identify problems in work processes and then use rigorous measurement to reduce variation and eliminate defects. When these types of initiatives become ingrained in a company's culture, as they did at 3M, creativity can easily get squelched. After all, a breakthrough innovation is something that challenges existing procedures and norms."

- George Buckley - former Chairman, President, and Chief Executive of 3M.

But instead of just trumping Lean Startup and bringing "the next great methodology," I'm integrating a fast-paced service design approach within the existent Lean Startup loop. This is what the **MVS—Minimum Valuable Service**, does, in an easy-to-use and well-structured framework.

This decision resonates with the purpose of design itself. As explained, design is not a specialization, nor is it a methodology. It is a maker's attitude toward problem solving, focused on value creation. Design was always meant to empower production methodologies, not the other way around.

THE MVP IS ALWAYS LATE

Chapter Ten

"Good design accelerates the adoption of new ideas."

— Yves Behar

If you are not familiar with the term MVP according to the Lean Startup, a minimum viable product (MVP) is a simplified, yet functional version of the solution a project team is trying to develop.

The main objective of a project team using the Lean Startup approach is to get to the MVP, a pilot prototype, then use this pilot as a bait to attract users. They then test the concept and gather feedback. After the MVP is tested, the project team goes back to the lab and into a dilemma face-off. At one side they can continue moving in the same direction, improving on what they already have. The other option is to pivot. The word "pivot" means to change the existing solution into something else that could generate more value to the users, and ultimately for the business itself.

The Lean Startup model also preaches that there are two hypotheses that need to be validated before the team decides whether to persevere or to pivot with their solution.

The first is the value hypothesis.

According to the Lean Startup, the value hypothesis tests whether the offer really delivers value to customers once they are using it.

The second is the growth hypothesis.

The growth hypothesis, on the other hand, focuses on testing the scalability potential of the business, or how new customers will discover it.

According to the Lean Startup, when the MVP falls short of one, or both, hypothesis validations, the project team needs to consider pivoting the idea.

In essence, the MVP is what designers call a late prototype, an avatar for the solution that acts like a "go to market" pilot. It's meant to be a learning device, built to take a beating in the marketplace and provide useful feedback for the team.

"Prototype" is a dear term to designers. It is by prototyping solutions that we are able to find our paths and reach the level of maturity needed to create high-impact innovative solutions. That being said, no designer wants to deploy a "go to market" pilot antenna based on an inside-out hypothesis, developed only on the project team's ideas and considerations. That is why designers often make use of an early prototyping and co-design technique called experience prototyping.

The experience prototyping approach is not the same as the MVP test bait approach. That is because it comes early in the project, opening the space to turn users into co-designers.

Early experience prototypes can be used in a project with three main goals:

1. Set the context for users to participate in idea generation and co-development.

2. A service enactment, or role-play, to explain or learn from a complex concept.

3. A test to validate specific service interactions, or the entire service journey.

This kind of prototype can take place in the very beginning of a project when the team is just playing around with the challenge, have no proposed solution and a marginal grasp of the problem they are facing. Because early prototypes are not "go to market" pilots, they do not carry the same "go to market" burden of the MVP.

Also, they help designers foresee critical barriers and issues and change the design approach in order to reach a better and more efficient "go to market" prototype.

Photo: NASA works at the Mars Desert Research Station, situated on the San Rafael Swell of southern Utah. This is a mission prototype to simulate Mars exploration. Not exactly the real thing, but definitely a way to anticipate issues and allow room for mistakes before launching.

In order to design a new concept for teenagers' bank accounts for a global bank, we signed a bunch of teenagers up for a mission. They had to walk around a room and sit on different tables with different actors playing the role of bank account managers. At each table they were told they were in a different period of their lives, which presented them with new challenges and rewards.

In less than an hour they went from their first kiss to being accepted to a university to their first job, marriage, promotion, children and so on.

Every time they entered a new table they received a card containing explanations about that specific moment of their lives and they had to discuss how the bank could be of help at that specific moment. They were helping us to generate a portfolio of offerings on the fly. In the end they joined our design team in a session where they re-visited each table portfolio of offers and helped the team create new possibilities, adjust the existing ones, and eliminate what didn't made sense according to their expectations.

Photo: Co-designing bank service offerings with teens via the use of experience prototypes.

Unlike an MVP, this early experience prototype took place before there was a closed concept. The team was definitely not at the stage to build a "go to market" pilot. Not even a simplified one, as there were no envisioned solutions yet.

As such, there was also no "persevere or pivot" question. Everything on the prototype was crude material ready to be built upon considering the user's perspectives and value perception.

These early co-design interactions function as confidence builders for the project team. They light the way for the team to keep building in the right direction. This raises the bar on the assertiveness and lessens the risk of failure. It also helps identify value-driven functionalities before investing time and energy in building useless attributes.

Before one thinks that this kind of prototyping technique is heavy on resources, the one described above was held while there was no system, no processes, no code—only a challenge and some ideas. No money was spent in anything else other than cardboard, snacks, and a little reward for the help of those who came to the session. It was all theatre, a good immersive play.

Photo/Fig: In the picture you can see some examples of the experience prototype media used during the co-design sessions.

I welcome late prototypes like the MVP, only they must come late in the project, not be the first learning antenna to connect with users, otherwise these prototypes would be the result of too much guesswork. Not only that, but a late prototype may not translate well into a source of insights, as they come already biased by materializing a direct attempt to solve the puzzle. This often creates a sandbox, limiting the gathering of user information to the context of the hypothesis being tested and casting a fog on new alternatives. That kind of late-only test approach can result in a huge waste of time, energy and money.

There's a misconception behind the passage in The Lean Startup book that says "no amount of design can anticipate the many complexities of bringing a product to life in the real world." Lots can go wrong when a user interacts with a service, and a great deal of those issues can be anticipated with co-design techniques like the one used in the banking account experience prototyping session.

Experience prototypes are a time-proven and reliable technique that allows for the team to find and push the right anthropomorphic buttons. It is a powerful design approach focused on unveiling early the cognitive patterns that are responsible for the value formation within the users' minds. In Part 2, I will walk you through the process of building experience prototypes.

The idea that you need to take care of viability first and then run tests to determine whether or not the proposal has value to the customer is wasteful. It is smarter to reverse this approach and anticipate what is valuable to people prior, and then go from there to refine the findings into viable models.

Let's face it: if you are really concerned about waste, then the first thing that you should be thinking of, in this economy, is how to create things that are valuable, because, if it is born with no value, then it is waste-by-design.

Without this mentality, startups are in the dark, shooting propositions and squandering lots of time and other valuable resources in the process.

Let me tell you a short story to illustrate the difference between the MVP—late prototyping—and the MVS—early prototyping—approaches.

Let's say your challenge is to give a birthday present to someone you just met.

The MVP approach:

1. Think about things you consider cool and that you can afford to buy.

2. Choose one.

3. Try and see if he/she likes it. If not, learn something and go back to step one.

"The heart of the scientific method is the realization that although human judgment may be faulty, we can improve our judgment by subjecting our theories to repeated testing."

— Eric Ries, **The Lean Startup:** *How Today's Entrepreneurs Use Continuous Innovation to Create Radically Successful Businesses*

The MVS approach:

1. Get a deeper knowledge about the way this person lives, works and relates to others.

2. Now, think about things that would be of good service to this person and that you can afford to buy.

3. Try and see if he/she likes it. If not, learn something and go back to step one.

Which approach do you think have the chance to hit the mark while burning less fuel?

In the MVS, the increased drag on the beginning (1) is compensated by the increased accuracy of the idea generation phase (2), which leads the team to create minimum offers that have more chance to stick and survive (3).

And then there is nuclear waste.

When a MVP hits the market and fails to be perceived as valuable by users, the team may feel compelled, or pushed, to pivot. That decision can indicate a catastrophic loss for the founders, investors and ultimately, the world—the discontinuity of a service offer that might otherwise have been a valuable contribution to society, but as for now is suffering with "learn, use and remember" issues. The waste of an Airbnb.com, for example.

This is the ultimate form of waste brought by the MVP model; I call it nuclear waste, as it hurts the core, the main purpose for the startup to be in business: It is the waste of a possible innovation.

Lots of MVPs hit the market with a poorly designed "learn, use and remember" journey. That is the reason why many ideas fail and are pivoted: not because they do not have their place in the world, but because consumers can't find out how to go about integrating them into their lives.

Human elements like anxiety, uncovered needs, irritability, belonging, mental models and value formation patterns play an immensely important role in how people choose, or don't, to adhere to a service. Those aspects can make or break the adoption of a service proposition. As such they are incredible insights to be discovered in the early stages when there's lots of room for deep surgery, and wicked bad news when uncovered only later.

Let's say you were hired to design a way for people in an African village to improve their access to water. Then you crystallize an MVP that is a bike built to easily transport water. How much of a waste would it be to discover, late in the project, that women in this village, according to their faith, are not allowed to drive vehicles of any kind? I conducted projects in Africa for two years, and I can assure you that this is the kind of information that doesn't come up in a Google search. This is a good example of a catastrophic failure trap ready to engulf an MVP, one that could be anticipated and avoided in the MVS model.

Photo: Immersed in a tribe in Namibia. Uncovered human behaviors can easily kill an MVP.

The scientific model is straightforward and linear. People are anything but straightforward.

What do you think is the first thing people do when they decide to sign up for a fitness center?

They go shop.

That's weird, right? It would be fair to say that they rethink their agendas, or that they go to a supermarket to start fixing their diets. Shopping for clothes is really not a smart thing when you are overweight.

Well, that is exactly what they do, according to an ethnographical study I conducted in 2008 involving the adoption of healthy habits.

The project involved a huge chain of fitness centers, and the team tracked their users' journeys from sitting on the couch and doing nothing to entering fitness centers and changing their routines and lives. We were interested in their first four months of engagement, and curious about what drives those who succeed and what kills the motivation of those who fail to achieve a frequent exercising habit.

In those kinds of immersion routines, we learn a lot about the way people think. We learn about their decision-making processes, and how they live, work and interact with others: what their fears are, what gives them strength and pleasure, and what brings them anxiety. We learn by having in-depth conversations with them as much as we learn by observing them walk (or not) their talks. Even though we are not presenting them with any kind of prototype, value is being added to the project development cycle.

Steve Blank, in his book *The Startup Owner's Manual,* proposes a validation cycle entitled "Customer Discovery," in which he divides the hypothesis validation process into four phases. Steve implies that a concept should be created "inside the building," but before the MVP is built the execution map for the concept should be validated with users "outside the building," using the Business Model Canvas. Steve also suggests that the project team can focus first on a low-fidelity MVP. This could take the form of a snapshot of the solution in its current state or even a splash page website containing the startup intentions.

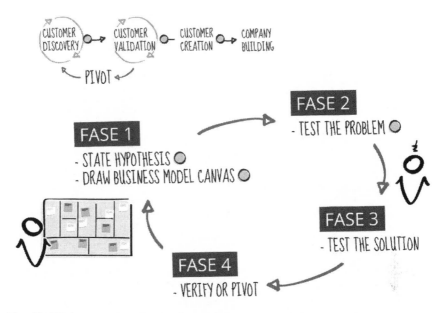

Photo/Fig: This is the model presented in Steve Blank's book, The startup Owners Manual

"In a startup, the founders define the product vision and then use customer discovery to find customers and a market for that vision."

— Steve Blank, *The Startup Owner's Manual*

That lessens the risk of failure of the MVP, as it shows possible users the plan before it is executed. Still, the Customer Discovery model carries the same premises of the scientific and "make and sell" approach.

- It constructs the hypothesis "inside the building." No co-design.

- It focuses only on early adopters, missing other service ecosystem actors, and only uses them as test subjects.

- It still lacks the focus and tools to uncover human variables early in the project, focusing on the validation of a direct attempt to solve the puzzle.

- It jumps to validate only transaction and feature-oriented variables of the business model, focusing on things like product attributes, price, revenue streams and possible customer segmentations.

- The business model canvas cannot be considered an experience prototype as it does nothing to immerse the user in the experience of using the service. As such, it is not a credible user feedback antenna. To trust a canvas as an early prototype is the equivalent of NASA deciding to simulate a mission to Mars using a spreadsheet.

- The MVP remains the first immersive prototype, a late one. Even if it is one of low fidelity, it remains late as it carries the purpose of validating a pre-conceived hypothesis. This is too late and too biased for co-design.

I have to credit Steve Blank for creating one more step to lessen the "go, no-go" burden of the MVP, and for suggesting low-fidelity prototyping interactions. That was clever. The problem here is that the scientific method is always inside-out, since a concept is developed internally and then tested with users. However, the way that we tend to think about a service performance in a meeting room is very different than the way the service performs in the real world.

Take a moment to try to think about all the steps that you execute when you do your dishes at home. No, really, do it now, name and number those steps. Good. Now, the next time you are actually doing the dishes, start taking note on how many steps there really are.

I bet you left dozens of crucial interactions out of the first mental rehearsal. Well, luckily that was not an exercise to create your startup business model.

THE MVS MODEL

———

Part Two

*"**Spoon boy**: Do not try and bend the spoon. That's impossible. Instead... only try to realize the truth.*

__Neo__: What truth?

__Spoon boy__: There is no spoon.

__Neo__: There is no spoon?

__Spoon boy__: Then you'll see that it is not the spoon that bends, it is only yourself."

— The Matrix

THE DESIGN PROCESS FOR THE NON-DESIGNER

———

Chapter Eleven

"A man who carries a cat by the tail learns something he can learn in no other way."

— Mark Twain

Maybe you've already heard of the Double Diamond, the ubiquitous representation of the design process. Composed of two connected diamond shapes, the diagram was proposed in 2005 by the United Kingdom Design Council as a visual representation for the way designers approach challenges.

The research that initiated the project took the form of an immersion in 11 different design-driven organizations, and the results would later confirm Edward de Bono's theory on lateral thinking. In the 1960s, Edward de Bono stated in his book *Lateral Thinking* that in order to trigger creativity, it is more useful to separate the moments when the team is generating concepts from the moments of the refinement and evaluation of those concepts. By approaching idea generation in this way, people have the freedom to imagine and create while still pursuing grounded and realistic outcomes.

This separation of creative "moods" is well represented by the Double Diamond diagram.

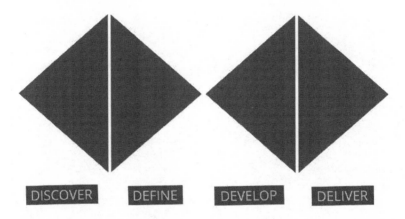

The Double Diamond is divided into 4 stages. The first, Discover (<), proposes a deep contextual dive in the challenge scenario. It is at this stage that designers use ethnographic techniques to figure out how people live, work, and relate within the context being studied.

Then we have the Define stage (>), in which the team refines and narrows the insights gathered, trying to see patterns and reach conclusions from the collected data.

Next, the team moves on to the Develop (<) stage, where ideas and prototypes are generated.

At the next stage, Deliver (>), the team focuses on additional refinements and adjustments, crafting more mature prototypes. The main objective here is to evolve the ideas into possible solutions and document them in a way they can be crystallized.

The Double Diamond is an abstract representation of what can happen inside a design-based project, but it should not be mistaken as a streamlined process. Designers play around with the diamond-shaped stages, intensifying or abandoning the use of tools and looping around them as the challenge evolves.

In its essence the design approach is thought to be an iterative process based on constant learning cycles. In that sense, it has many similarities with the Lean Startup approach.

Charles and Ray Eames are by far my favorite designers of all time. The American couple pioneered the idea of escaping the industrial design bubble in order to design more holistic experiences. Their attitude toward designing whole ecosystems can be seen in their work for IBM during the '50s. Arguably, most of what we know about modern-day design agencies, including their inspirational and fun work environments, originated at their studio in Venice Beach, California.

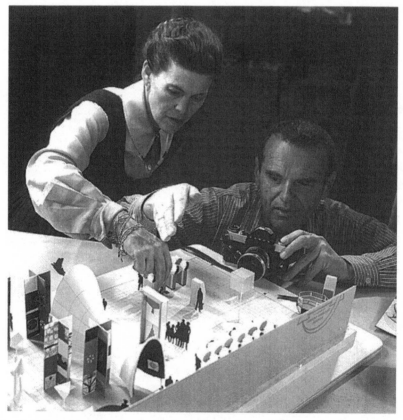

Photo: An early prototype featuring the user's journey at what would become the IBM's Mathematica Exhibition in 1960 by Charles and Ray Eames.

As opposed to the scientific method, which has all its procedures and stages figured out before the kick-off of the project and which progresses incrementally, designers like Charles and Ray never follow an input/output process in order to innovate, because we simply believe there isn't one.

Not only that, but it's an unreasonable expectation to have as most ideas that have lasting impact on people's lives are a result of unorthodox mash-ups and bold moves.

In the case of Charles and Ray Eames, this included sending their project teams to photograph circus spectacles, with the mission to document the colorful atmospheres and their myriad of details. The team would then come back, unveil the photos, and pin them on the walls as sources of inspiration for projects. With this story in mind, from now on every time you see their work you might somehow sense this unexpected and rich influence on their designs.

Ok, so this was a short explanation of the Double Diamond process. I acknowledge that it was brief, but it's really everything you need to know before we move deeper into the MVS model. If you are still eager to learn more about the Double Diamond, please refer to the original study made by the Design Council UK; there is a link to it in the references section of this book.

Photo/Fig: Just like Charles and Ray, startups at Eise prototype their users' journeys.

THANKS FOR YOUR SERVICE MVP. WELCOME MVS

―――――

Chapter Twelve

"Design is crucially important. We can't have advances in technology any longer, unless design is integrated from the very start."

— John Underkoffler, User interface designer. Minority Report science adviser and interface creator

As you may have noticed, I'm proposing a change in the acronym from MVP—minimum viable product—to MVS—minimum valuable service. The idea behind this change is rooted in the conceptual issues and conflicts that I pointed out in Part 1 of this book.

When service design enters the Lean Startup, bringing its outside-in perspective, the scientific perspective characterized by the MVP evolves to accommodate new lenses and intentions.

The implied emphasis on technology and internal resources (**Viable**) evolves to a human-centric orientation (**Valuable**), and its **Product** inclination shifts to the more adequate **Service** logic.

Minimum (inheritance: Agile)

There's no need to propose another mindset for startups than one that is laser-focused on the minimum offer. So in that sense, Lean Startup nailed it. This is the perfect mindset for operating with low resources, and now even in scenarios with high resources. The power of quickly getting to a minimum offer is preserved and leveraged in the MVS model.

Viable to Valuable. (inheritance: Design)

A viable service that serves no one is simply another huge form of waste.

The change in the V represents the capacity of design to deeply connect to users' needs and desires, empowering the team to propose valuable solutions. It's been established already that it is more efficient to have the team focused on value creation instead of having viability as the guiding mission of the project. Viability definitely still comes into play, but only later on. Considerations of viability will help the team refine its generated concepts and find ways to bring real solutions to life.

Product to Service (inheritance: Service-dominant logic)

Well, this one should be clear by now. We are not in the 20th century "make and sell" economy anymore and can't operate within its narrow and linear standards. This modification is here to remind the project team that their focus needs to be shifted from the transaction driven "make and sell" inclination to the "learn, use and remember" service-oriented model. As Bauhaus professor Moholy-Nagy would have put it, thinking in relationships.

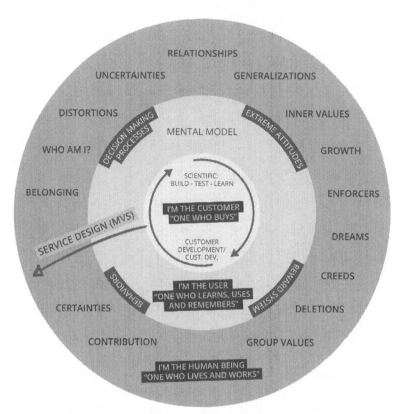

Photo/Fig: In the MVS, service design expands the scope of the investigation to reveal insights that are outside the transactional point of view.

Photo/fig: The Samsung T9000, a Wi-Fi-enabled smart fridge that allows users to Tweet via a touchscreen. It retails for USD 4,000. A good example of what is viable but not valuable whatsoever.

MVS IN LARGE ORGANIZATIONS

Chapter Thirteen

"Control is the wrong word. The practice is very much about sharing, and, in any creative practice, some individuals, whether partners or directors, are much closer to certain projects than I could ever be."

— Norman Foster

In the years between 1994 and 2003, the Design Council UK put together a stock index of 63 different companies famous for using design in their product development routines. They called it "The Design Index," and an analysis of its results during this 10-year period showed that it performed 200% better than the FTSE-100 index, the index of the 100 most valuable companies.

Considering this tangible return on investment, eleven years later, why is design still not integrated into the strategy of every corporation?

The answer is risk aversion.

For a startup, variation and failure are part of the daily routine. There's no success without learning; as every investor and founder knows, there's more to learn from failure than by getting it right on the first try. For this reason, investors are always looking to get a solid impression of the founders, as they are the ones in charge of quickly moving from one idea to the next when things don't turn out as expected.

Large corporations have a contrasting set of beliefs.

Most organizational leaders work hard to reduce variation as an attempt to minimize their risk of failure.

When unexpected results arise, the organizational mantra is always to put together a PowerPoint presentation that explains why things didn't end up as planned. In most cases, a finger-pointing blame game follows suit.

This has two known consequences. The first is executives who want to keep fighting for change will, of course, just keep making mistakes. There is no other way to break with the status quo. The problem is that many of those mistakes will be swept under the corporate carpet in an attempt to avoid the blame game.

This behavior is driven by fear, and prevents organizations from collectively learning from their mistakes.

Other executives will adopt a more drastic approach to dodging the witch-hunt: they will stop trying.

Realizing that the prize lies in maintaining the status quo and that there are major risks to questioning it, most executives will settle down and lose their appetite for change.

These behaviors form a chain of reactions that end up intoxicating the entire corporate culture, ultimately creating a stagnant organization that freezes when confronted with disruptive ideas.

This is all supported by the fact that big brands have a lot to lose when something goes wrong with a new launch.

Truthfully, one can argue that the division running the launch could be spun-off from the main organizational structure under a different brand name. This is definitely one way to minimize risks; but still, if Nike decides to try a new product under a new independent brand identity, how long do you think it'll take until the truth is all over social media?

Their C-level executives think the same. Considering this constant threat of brand erosion, they tend to assume, not without good reason, that the risks of going to the market with an unfinished product are too high.

This is an enormous barrier, making it difficult for organizations to fully adopt the Lean Startup, late-prototyping approach.

Still, corporations need to learn a way to be agile and play around with short experimentation cycles. The MVS can have a huge role in allowing space for this to happen as it utilizes the power of design. This translates into the ability to integrate **empathy-building techniques**, **co-design**, and **early prototyping practices** in the development process, which minimizes risk aversion and fosters the creation of more mature "go to market" pilots.

THE MVS STRUCTURE

—

Chapter Fourteen

"A designer is an emerging synthesis of artist, inventor, mechanic, objective economist and evolutionary strategist."

— R. Buckminster Fuller

Ok, enough said. Let's get to it.

I've split the MVS in two different moods. A mood is a frame of mind, one that the project team needs to adopt in order to use the tools and approaches presented in each stage of the MVS.

The two moods are: Humanize and Crystallize.

Humanize steers the focus of the project team away from the technology and toward humanistic variables by immersing the team within the "learn, use and remember" aspects of the user journey. In the Humanize mood, the team will project themselves into the shoes of others and co-design perspectives along with potential users. This mood is about empathy-building and co-designing, and its two steps are Humanize::Projection and Humanize::Perspectives.

Crystallize, on the other hand, is when the refinement variables and business constraints come into play. Remember, the project team needs to be on the correct path to creating possible solutions, things that are of value but can also be crystallized into real-world solutions. The mood Crystalize allows the team to play around with experience prototypes aimed at fostering discussions around value and viability. Its two steps are Crystallize::Playground and Crystallize::Polish Off.

Humanize: **Projection, Perspectives**

Crystallize: **Playground, Polish Off**

In order to accommodate the design process into the Agile loop of the Lean Startup, I merged the two diamonds into one. This alleviates resource consumption and works, considering that the Lean Startup is an iterative approach. This means that the team will keep spinning the wheel, repeating the MVS "one diamond" as many times as they feel they need to. Considering that, we actually end up with infinite diamonds, not just one. A collateral effect is that this also fixes the "streamline" linear impression left by the double diamond shape.

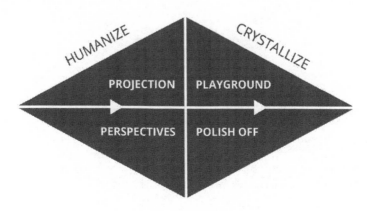

Also, in the Lean Startup the diamond was placed under the "Learn" stage. The reason for that is because the design approach is a continuous learning process. Every tool or technique used by designers is aimed at improving their knowledge about the challenge they are facing.

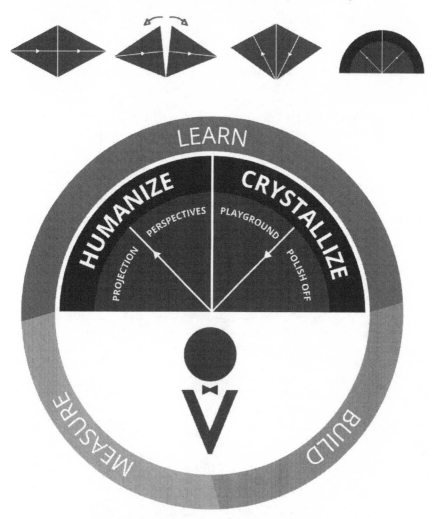

I've named this visual representation of the process: The MVS clock. You may also have noted that I use the "::" indication when I am referring to one of the four internal P's (projection, perspectives, playground, polish off). This is very common notation to PHP object-oriented programmers, and in simple terms means that the object that ends the sentence inherits from the object that initiates it. So what I mean by that is:

Humanize::Projection -> The Projection step inherits the characteristics of the mood Humanize.

The MVS is not limited to the Lean Startup. It was built to be combined with any iterative fast-paced approach, including all the Agile spin-offs like Scrum, Rapid Development, and others. Over the next chapters, I will walk you through the "HowTos" of the model. This part of the book will give you everything you need to run a project from scratch with the MVS model.

The model can be adjusted to work within fast paced project schedules. Each project cycle can be as short as four days long, like what we do at servicedesignsprints.com. But keep in mind cycles can also be extended to fit within lengthier project agendas.

It is worth mentioning that you are free to use the techniques and approaches contained in this book in any sequence you feel like. Nevertheless, I recommend that you first try following the suggested path in order to get enough confidence in the model and better learn the "whys" behind each technique.

I suggest you download the MVS workbooks in order to better navigate the next chapters. You will find the link to it in the Toolkit section of this book.

Keep in mind there is only one rule that you cannot break and that is: After you craft the MVS journey, you have to build it and go live! The MVS is a maker's approach. It's not for the faint-hearted dreamer.

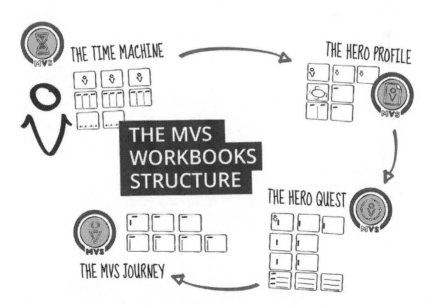

Photo/Fig: A scheme showing the usual MVS workbooks pathway during design sprints.

HUMANIZE :: PROJECTION

"You think the only people who are people, are the people who look and think like you. But if you walk the footsteps of a stranger, you'll learn things you never knew you never knew."

— *Pocahontas*

Humanize::Projection is about getting into other people's shoes in order to see the world with their eyes. During the Humanize::Projection stage, the project team will uncover untapped barriers, needs, and desires, understand mental models, and get a sense of the user "learn, use and remember" journey.

THE TIME MACHINE

Workbook: The Time Machine

Target: v (valuable)

There's no better way to start a project than to look for references and clues about the challenge being faced from the past, present and in the future.

The Time Machine workbook is the entry point of the MVS model. It is a desk research investigation on steroids. This workbook is designed to help the project team gather more knowledge about the ecosystem surrounding the issue they are addressing.

It invites the project team to take a step back. Instead of jumping into conclusions and directly moving to the drawing board, the team here will search for a more holistic point of view and deep-dive into the contextual forces surrounding the issue they face.

This contextual map of the challenge will shine a light on the way the customer has dealt with the issue in the past, is dealing with it today, and will probably address it in the future.

Time Machine is not about troubleshooting in an attempt to find the cure. It is about acting like you don't have a cure and are trying to understand how people have been and will be able to continue to relate to the issue without it.

PART 1: The desk research.

1) Split your team into **Yesterday**, **Today** and **Tomorrow** units. Ideally each person should be responsible for researching only one period.

2) During their desk research, each team needs to be able to richly answer the following questions:

- What are the main reasons why people experience the driving issue behind the project?

People will do things either to avoid pain or to pursue pleasure. Every user choice or behavior tends to be rooted within this mechanism called the Human Reward system. Find out about the forces driving the issue.

- How have people been dealing with it? How have they done so in the past? How are they likely to do it in the future?

It doesn't matter if you already have a pre-conceived idea about how your solution is going to look; you should work on the Time Machine workbook considering only the options available to users.

- What activities and exchanges are performed, by which actors, and how?

In every context, individuals will always rely on other **people, objects, channels, digital manifestations or processes** *to interact with the world and navigate it in order to solve problems. This is about how they go about it, and with whom/what they interact with in this process.*

- How value was/is/will be exchanged?

As I said in Part I, a service is a favor that is exchanged based on an economic or emotional currency. In this case, what are the values being traded? Is it perceived as fair to the people involved?

PART 2: The download.

1) Draw the service ecosystem. Around the user, draw the relations and exchanges that are experimented by the user.

2) How do people "learn, use and remember" about their issues and evaluate their options at each given period?

Learn:

- This is an exploration of how people learn about their issues, scanning existing solutions, fixes and connecting to other people facing the same challenge. Share a story about your findings here.

Use:

- How do people deal with it? Is there a solution that addresses the issue? How does it work? Share a story about your findings here.

Remember:

- How do people remember their experiences? Positively or negatively? What kind of stories do they tell others? Are they proud after performing the task? Does it meet their needs and expectations? Do they keep their experience to themselves or spread the word about it? How and why? Share a story about your findings here.

3) Market Potential (to be filled out later)

- Leave this part for now. We will revisit it later on, in the last stage of the MVS.

The Time Machine workbook is an amazing starting point for any project, as it helps the team contextualize the problem from a holistic perspective. Designers are known for their ability to step back in order to take a moment to reflect and grasp the bigger picture. The Time Machine workbook will help the project team accomplish that.

Make sure you keep the Time Machine workbook up-to-date and visible during the whole project.

SUPP

SPRINT ETHNOGRAPHY

Workbook: Supporting materials

Well, first let's demystify the term "ethnography."

Ethnography is the name given to the act of studying human behavior using the perspectives of the people being studied instead of the point of view of the researcher. The study usually takes place where the behavior occurs, with the researcher's presence minimized by specific techniques in order to avoid the bias caused by observer effects, also known as the Hawthorne effect: a form of reactivity in which subjects modify an aspect of their behavior in response to the fact that they know that they are being studied.

Photo: The first ethnographic study took place in the Trobriand Islands during World War I. It was developed by Professor Bronislaw Malinowski. The study served as a basis for his book, "Argonauts of the Western Pacific."

Designers make good use of ethnographic studies, as these contextual approaches are good sources of knowledge about how users live, work and solve problems.

There are three ethnographic steps in the MVS: **Sprint Ethnography**, **Cast a Shadow** and **In-depth conversation**.

The Sprint Ethnography technique was designed to engage the team in a round of quick interviews with real potential stakeholders.

In a sprint ethnography, the project team will behave like journalists, talking in face-to-face conversations with a large number of people over the issue without getting too in-depth.

The results of the Sprint ethnography will enrich the Time Machine workbook and also be used as a starting point for the team to define the next steps of the project.

PART 1: The field research.

1) Based on the discoveries <u>and</u> assumptions registered in the Time Machine canvas, write down key things you may want to explore or discuss with people. To better organize your sprint, employ three different card-like papers, each one representing one aspect of the user journey: learn, use and remember. You can also use the suggested template that you will find on the supporting materials workbook.

Learn:

Write down 3 questions to gather what the users already know, how they learn about it, and how they become better and/or more proficient in dealing with the issue.

Use:

Write down 3 questions about their experiences using the available alternatives. If there's no available alternative, ask them about how they are addressing their needs and desires. If they aren't, ask them what would be an ideal way to do so.

Remember:

Write down 3 questions about how people remember their experiences, what are the feelings and sensations left after they engage with it, and what they tend to do about it afterward. Do they tell others? Are they willing to help others deal with it?

2) Get out of the building and go sprint. Use your cards to better navigate the conversations and talk with as many interesting people as you can, registering their points of view on quick notes.

Remember to act as a journalist and try to get the user perspective about those questions in a 5- to 10-minute conversation. At this point a user can be anyone who has a role in the ecosystem described in the Time Machine workbook. Users are not only customers, but also actors, people who interact with the service ecosystem.

Don't worry in getting too deep into topics yet; we will cover deeper conversations on the In-depth conversation step.

Some hints for a great Sprint Ethnography:

- Take notes. There's no need to record the conversations. A recording would consume too much time to go through later. Instead, write down your observations.

- Take a picture of the person you spoke with and thank them for the time.

- Before engaging in the next conversation, make sure you register up to 3 things that caught your attention while talking to that specific person, and list it under the user's name.

PART 2: The download.

1) Get back to the building and organize all the information collected.

For each user you interviewed, create a space like the one in the picture (below) to download all the information. Remember to keep it simple and easy to navigate. Also, always use a physical space: don't go digital yet, that way everybody on the team can benefit from the quick interviews.

THE HERO PROFILE

Workbook: The Hero Profile

Target: v (valuable)

"Everybody is special. Everybody. Everybody is a hero, a lover, a fool, a villain. Everybody. Everybody has their story to tell."

— Alan Moore, *V for Vendetta*

Heroes are stereotypes of extreme users.

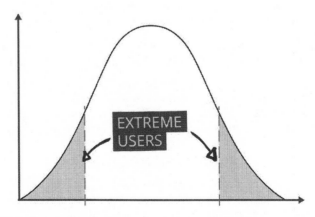

Fig: IDEO's model to illustrate extreme users.

By looking at the challenge through the eyes of extreme users, the team is able to forge a deeper holistic perspective about the problem being faced.

This is not to say that extreme users will be the only ones to benefit from the final solution—of course not. But their extreme behaviors and opinions carry the richest stories.

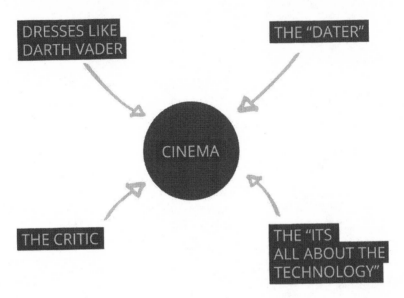

Photo/Fig: Examples of extreme users.

In the MVS, we call them heroes, as they are incredible figures deeply affected by the issues the team is trying to learn about.

A hero is someone who is able to remember concealed details and walk you through vivid specifics about their struggles and experiences.

Similar to the cinema example, the goal is to create heroes that are different from each other. Also, aim to have 3-5 heroes. If you end up having more than that, explore similarities and combine some of them. This will help the team develop a deep understanding about each stereotype.

Stereotyping.

The activities below are related to column A of the Hero Profile workbook. They cover the global definitions of the hero.

1) Search through the information already gathered, looking for behavioral patterns, things that people think, feel and do.

2) Have a discussion with your team about the actual findings and try to come out with some cool stereotypes from this discussion. Go wild, and don't worry, we will test the accuracy of the stereotypes you create later on.

Hints:

Brainstorm possible actions that the extreme users may perform. A good example of actions in a project for a travel agency would be:

"That guy who ..."

- Plans the trip like a mission.

- Doesn't like to plan anything.

- Acts like a travel maestro.

- Doesn't spend more than 2 days in the same city.

- Spends weeks in the same city.

Now combine the actions in groups that are similar between in each other and may represent a hero.

Typical   Heroes   that   could   come   out   of   it:

The jumper

Actions: He visits 7 countries in 7 days, likes to post tourist attraction selfies on Facebook (...)

The Bucolic traveler

Actions: He spends 20 days in 1 city, disconnects completely while traveling (...)

The travel maestro

Actions: He acts like a maestro, planning everything all the time and making sure the whole group sticks to the plan (...)

3) Mental model

A **mental model** is an explanation of someone's thought process about how something works in the real world. Mental models can help shape behavior and set an approach to solving problems and doing tasks.

In the center, write down the hero mental model relating to the issue being faced.

E.g.

The jumper

"To stay for more than two days in the same city is a waste of time. "

The bucolic traveler

"If you can't sit and read a book in a place, you have never been there for real."

The travel maestro

"Vacation in Europe? Dude, you will need a solid strategy."

The spots around the center are there so you can write down user's thoughts and extreme actions you noticed while in the field that somehow help sustain the mental model.

E.g.

The jumper

"I love to take selfies in hot places."

The bucolic traveler

"I like to meet new people when traveling."

The trip maestro

"I print all the tickets."

4) Opportunities and Barriers

Write down opportunities and barriers related to the Hero.

It is ok to leave some blank parts of the Hero Profile for now and complete the workbook later, as the knowledge about real users' behaviors and mental models increase.

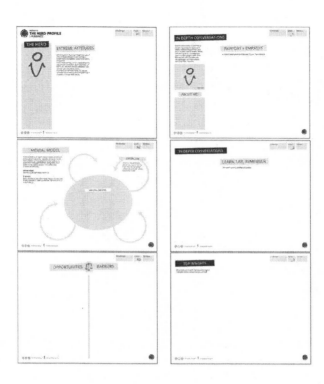

INVOKE YOUR HEROES

Workbook: Supporting materials

Now it is time to test the heroes and see how they compare to the extreme users of the real world. The users recruited here will take part on the Cast a shadow and In-depth conversations steps.

Invoke your hero-like users.

1) Set up a recruitment strategy to fish for hero-like users. A good strategy is to aim for 3-4 extreme users for each Hero profile you may have.

There are numerous ways to recruit hero-like users. The quickest and most effective is to use your network of friends and family. After all, chances are that you already have direct or indirect access to these people that you need to meet.

You can also try an approach I call The Hero Quiz, a survey designed to cast a wide net on social media in search of heroes.

The Hero Quiz

Considering all the characteristics of the heroes, create a quick survey with questions that can help you understand to what extent respondents correlate with your heroes.

Make sure it is fun to interact with and that you ask indirect questions. Good examples of indirect and correlational questions can be found in quizzes in magazines for teenagers.

Be lean—keep it shorter than 10 questions. In the end, don't forget to ask if the respondent is willing to participate in the project:

"Are you willing to participate in a project that will change the way people _____ ? (Yes)(No)(Maybe)" (Put your challenge in the blank)

This question informs you about users willing to collaborate either conditionally or unconditionally with the project.

Use social platforms like Twitter and Facebook to make the link to the survey go viral.

As a last resource, you can also hire a recruitment firm. This only applies if your project involves a specific situation that makes it too difficult to use the existing project team networks.

Important:

Sometimes a hero may not translate well into reality, making it hard to recruit users that share similarities with the stereotype. In those cases, revisit the stereotyped hero and change or adjust some of its characteristics based on what you learned by trying to recruit users. It is all iterative.

SUPP

IN-DEPTH CONVERSATION

Workbook: Supporting materials

In-depth conversation is an ethnographic technique aimed at providing the team with a deeper understanding of their users' points of views, mental models, reward and belief systems. This technique will leave the team with valuable insights and deep stories about their hero-like users.

* The activities described here come after you have invoked your hero-like users. If you did not recruited users yet, you may want to check step 4 of Humanize::Projection.

PART 1: The preparation.

1) Take a moment to write down all the topics and insights in need of deeper clarification. These can be curiosities and key insights you might have gathered while in the field. Brainstorm some questions with your team and divide the questions into the three conversation flow rings.

Photo/Fig: The conversation flow rings.

The Rapport and Empathy ring

Nothing beats a conversation starter. Asking people about things that matter to them will help you create rapport and earn their confidence. It also will help the team understand belief systems and decision-making processes not directly related to the challenge.

Examples of questions that go into the Rapport and Empathy Ring:

- Tell me a little about you, what do you do for a living, hobbies, etc.?

- Why did you choose this neighborhood?

- Tell me a story about something you love/last time you had an incredibly fun time...

The learn, use and remember ring

Now organize the learn, use and remember questions. Examples of questions that go into the learn, use and remember ring:

- Tell me what excites you about traveling.

- When does a trip really start for you?

- Walk me through the things you do when planning a trip.

The Waste Ring

Use the waste ring to get rid of some questions. Questions that go here will not be addressed during this round. Leave them in the waste circle for now and, after getting back from the field, check if their absence made a difference or not. By leaving them here instead of really ditching them, you are creating the opportunity to use them in a next round of interviews.

PART 2: Hit the road

1) Write down the topics you want to cover in a notebook or piece of paper. In the supporting materials workbook you will find a template that you can also use to register your conversation topics.

Do not format the final topics as questions. Leave them as topics and areas you will want to cover; this makes for a better and more fluid conversation.

2) Constantly check the conversation flow rings and, if needed, improve the rings' information in such a way that the rest of the team can also benefit from it and make adjustments in their fieldwork activities.

By the end of this step you should be able to easily finish or update every placeholder on the Hero Profile.

Again, do not hesitate to adjust your Hero personalities based on your discoveries in the field.

CAST A SHADOW

Workbook: Supporting materials

Shadowing is an ethnographic approach that allows the team to follow and observe users while they perform tasks. The shadow watches, takes notes and pictures of what the user does and how they do it. Also, a good practice sometimes is to ask the user to think out loud while performing the tasks; this way you can map some of the users' thoughts, intentions and mental models.

* The activities described here come after you have invoked your hero-like users. If you did not recruited users yet, you may want to check step 4 of Humanize::Projection.

Casting the shadow.

1) The goal here is to observe hero-like users while they perform their journeys. Make sure you keep a comfortable distance and pay special attention to the users' "learn, use and remember" journeys.

For each intention, avatar or interaction you notice, ask yourself:

- Why?

- Where?

- When?

- How?

E.g.

Learn

- "Why, Where, When, How" ... do they discover where the check-in kiosk is?

- "Why, Where, When, How"... do they learn what to do first (touch the screen, insert their passport...)

- "Why, Where, When, How"... do they ask for assistance?

Use

- Do they travel back and forth on menus? "Why, Where, When, How?"

- Do they perceive the interaction with the machine as fast or slow? "Why, Where, When, How?"

- Are there struggles in the user journey? "Why, Where, When, How?"

Remember

- What are the results of the interaction? Are there physical objects? Digital manifestations? ... "Why, Where, When, How?"

- What type of information does the user own after using the service? "Why, Where, When, How?"

- How they remember it?

Cast a shadow checklist:

- If you have previously agreed with your hero-like users on performing the shadowing activities, give them a set of tasks. (E.g. Buy a light bulb, check-in and go to your room)

- Take notes. Do not trust your memory. Really, don't.

- Do not interrupt the users while they are performing their tasks. If you asked them to think out loud, just listen. Only talk with them at the end. Ok, sometimes it may be helpful to ask them questions during the performance, however, be aware that this can be distracting to them and plan accordingly.

Good after-shadowing conversation bits:

- So, how do you think it went? ... Why do you think so? And why is that? ... I understand.

- Does the service help you in any way? ... How? And why is that?

- I took a note that says: "could not easily find the card slot." Does this reflect what happened? ... Interesting... and why is that? ...

- Now... looking back to what you just did, what do you consider the highest and lowest points in using the service? ... Interesting, why?

- Let's assume for a second you are the designer of this service: what would you do differently? ... Why?... tell me more about this...

Important:

On pre-agreed shadowing routines, reward your hero-like users.

A reward can be a pizza feast, tickets to a local movie theater, a small amount of money, or any other inexpensive perks your hero-like users may feel attracted to. Keep your costs down, but also make your users happy. You will need their help later on.

You can use the Hero profile workbook and the Hero Quest to register the insights found during the Cast a Shadow step.

Photo/Fig: Key insights gathered during the Cast a Shadow step.

THE HERO QUEST

Workbook: The Hero Quest

Target: vs (valuable, service)

Every hero has a quest.

A Quest is a representation of the current journey of your extreme users, a representation of the way people are solving their problems today, before they know anything about your solution.

The Hero Quest workbook is about the existing avatars, intentions and thoughts users have access to while performing their journeys. It is a great way to visualize your users' current "learn, use and remember" journeys.

Map the Quest using the insights gathered during the ethnographic steps.

1) First, define the Quest's moments.

What you will register here are the moments of peoples' lives when they deal with these issues. Somehow they are solving them, right? Or they are at least addressing them in some way. Aim for that and describe the moments they go through in order to deal with the issues.

E.g.

Decide to go for a trip, talk with friends, start planning, reservations, pre-trip arrangements (…)

2) For each moment, document existing avatars, user's intentions and thoughts on the learn, use and remember swim lanes. If different heroes have different journeys, choose a different colored Post-it note to represent actions related to each hero.

3) For every moment defined, draw the USE—Usefulness, Satisfaction, Ease of Use—chart.

You can choose to use different colors for each hero, or to draw only one chart with all of the heroes' perceptions combined.

For the service design enthusiast.

Yep. I've killed the Line of Visibility.

If you are familiar with user journeys and service blueprints, you will notice that there is no Line of Visibility on the Hero Quest, nor on the MVS journey.

This was intentional, and here are some of the reasons why:

***First**, we are moving into an arena of interaction where there is no clear wall blocking visibility anymore. In many business scenarios, nothing physically separates supporting staff from the customer-facing employees. Just think about open-concept kitchens in trendy restaurants, meal preparation areas on airplanes or the instant checkout guy who stands in the middle of the store, not behind the counter, at an Apple Store.*

***Secondly**, accepting there's no Line of Visibility shows a commitment in designing interactions for your employees with the same care you do for your customers. Just remember, your employees will treat your customers the way they themselves are treated.*

This influences the creation of more empathetic internal processes and the commitment of a more ethical, participative and humanized integration between customer-facing employees, supporting staff and business executives.

*The **Third** reason is that to draw a Line of Visibility is the same as saying that a service has actions that are "visible" and "not visible," when in fact we know that all the five cognitive channels, not only the user's vision, are involved in the service performance. So to call something the "Line of Visibility" drives the conception of services that are without smells, touch, sound, or taste.*

These arguments were explored in more detail in chapter six, "The mirror of visibility."

HUMANIZE :: PERSPECTIVES

"There are no facts, only interpretations."

— Friedrich Nietzsche

You should by now have a whole new level of empathy and understanding about possible users and other actors in the service ecosystem, which is cool, but this information is only powerful if we actually put it to use. Welcome to Humanize::Perspectives, the ideation phase of the MVS.

It's about time we combine the project team's ideas, which are probably already popping up, with the perspectives of hero-like users. The goal here is to get the project team to co-design with users, generating valuable service propositions.

INTAKE

Intake is about breathing in everything that's been accumulated up until this moment in the project. Nothing beats a moment to step back and get a birds-eye view on all the information gathered. This is a moment for every member of the team, including the ones not involved in field research activities, to navigate through all the workbooks, exchanging stories and perspectives.

If possible, take one full day just to Intake. Make use of this time to discuss findings with other team members and look for patterns, connectors and things that stand out from the workbooks.

Sometimes key insights are revealed not in the moment they are gathered, but later on, when the team is able to see how they fit within the bigger picture.

SUPP

SWAP

Workbook: Supporting materials

Swap is the best co-design technique I know of. How do I know that? Because I've created it after trying dozens of others.

Being a hypnotherapist and a facial micro-expression specialist myself, I could not help but notice that, in co-participative design sessions, outspoken users sometimes ate shy users alive, to the point that the latter would restrain from collaborating. People who are not as articulate and comfortable in publicly expressing themselves can get really stressed out during co-participative sessions.

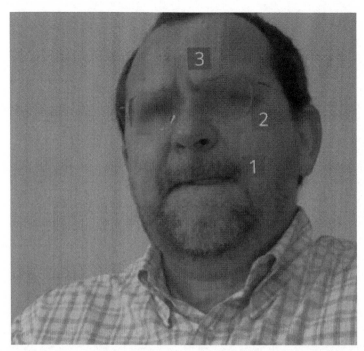

Photo/Fig: A user during a co-creation session constantly showing strong signs of stress while interacting with other users. Lips are missing (1), the eyelids are contracted (2), and the glabella, the skin between the eyebrows and above the nose, is pulled down (3).

After dealing with this situation many times, I took on the challenge to design a co-creation dynamic that would draw out the best of both types of personalities, balancing the contributions of outspoken and shy users.

The Swap technique was developed from mixing moments of individual and collective idea generation, while nevertheless still engaging users in a collaborative set of activities.

Photo/Fig: The same user performing an individual task. All signs of stress are gone.

Since the Swap ideation was born, Livework's project teams have been applying the technique on many different challenges with a great deal of success, regardless of the personalities that are in the mix.

PART 1: Prepare.

1) Make sure you have 4-8 hero-like users. Split them into groups and add members of the project team to each group in such a way that project team members remain a minority. You will need at least 2 groups of 3 to 6 people each.

2) Make sure each group has proper materials, such as colored pens, crayons, paper, scissors, etc. It helps if you use fun art materials like the ones children use to draw. That will help get participants in a more creative state of mind.

3) Prompt the groups by asking each person what I call an affect-bridge question. Affect-bridge is a hypnosis technique used during regression sessions. Basically, it is about triggering current emotions, suggesting that the patient time-travels into their past to the source where the emotion possibly originated.

We will use an approach inspired by this technique to take the participants back to a time when they were free to create, take risks and make mistakes.

Here are some good "affect-bridge" questions. Feel free to use any of them or to create your own.

"Every child **has** a preferred treat. I wonder if you can remember yours."

"Every child **has** a preferred board game. I wonder if you can remember yours."

Format:

[Every child has a preferred] _____. [I wonder if you can remember yours]."

A breakdown for the mind-freak enthusiast:

Note that the verb "has" is in the present tense. This is a trick to help the question appeal to the user's current inner child. At the same time, in the second sentence I do not offer the user a different verbal tense; instead, I move onto a challenge ("I wonder if"), and suggest the recovery of a memory from when they were a child.

I also chose to challenge, instead of giving a direct order. This is because it's a great way to permissively get people to engage. When challenged, people will often raise their engagement levels and are more likely to react positively to the suggestion, compared to when they are given a direct order or request.

As you can see, I love hypnosis, because it helps me to better communicate my ideas and connect with people. But let's move on: just pick a warm-up question and use it as a kick-off for the co-design practice.

Note: You can also use anything else you like as a warm-up. However, I always avoid wigs, balloons and other creativity-booster clichés. Some users tend to get very uncomfortable with them.

PART 2: Playing the game.

1) Reveal the challenge.

"How might we [create something] that helps people [do something better, stop a pain, get what they desire...]?"

"How might we create a travel service that helps people collectively plan their trips?"

2) Now, give them time to generate ideas alone.

Give the participants 10 minutes to register their ideas on paper individually. One idea per sheet.

Ask them not to dwell too much on the ideas, just to get them out of their heads and onto the paper and move to another one. Participants should aim for quantity here.

3) Swap.

Choose a user to start the swap round. This is actually pretty simple. Here is how it works:

Each user will have 1 minute to explain one of their ideas to the group. The group then will have 10 minutes to work collectively on the presented idea, improving it and taking it to another level.

Hints:

- Suspend all judgment. Ideas are not being presented to be judged or sold, but worked upon. It doesn't matter what it is; the question should be how to make it better.

- Have one group member responsible for the clock. After time expires, move clockwise to the next user, to have them pitch another idea.

- Repeat this process until everyone has had their #1 idea pitched and co-designed with all the other participants. After a successful full round, every idea on the table should feel like it belongs to everyone.

If you have the time, tell the participants to start a new round, with each user presenting their #2 idea, and so on.

Photo/Fig: Swap ideation. Users generate ideas for an "industry to consumer" new service.

THE HERO'S PITCH

Workbook: Supporting materials

Now it is time to test the stickiness and rationale behind the generated ideas.

1) After the Swap rounds, give each group 15 minutes to wrap-up and work on a pitch for each generated concept.

2) Afterward, each group will have 2-5 minutes to pitch each of their final concepts. Only hero-like users can pitch.

There are two rules in the Hero's Pitch:

Rule #1: Presenters are playing the role of founders. They are there to defend their concepts with all they've got.

Rule #2: The rest of the audience is playing the other side of the table, usually occupied by investors and critics. As such, they need to offer some skepticism and ask reality-check questions.

During the Hero's Pitch, the project team has the opportunity to sit back, listen, and learn.

Great knowledge is to be gained out of these crossfire exercises. Watching users criticize or defend their own ideas can help surface valuable insights about what these people really value and what they don't.

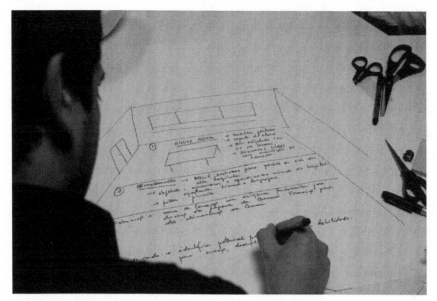
Photo/Fig: Some final touches before pitching the idea.

CRYSTALLIZE :: PLAYGROUND

Sir Jony Ive, Apple's legendary designer and creator of the iMac, iPod and iPhone, is famous for his constant and numerous early prototyping iterations.

Crystallize::Playground is serious play. Here, the team will develop and test concepts in order to refine them into solutions.

However, instead of taking the scientific approach to testing, the project team will engage users in experience prototypes—early-stage simulations aimed at immersing users into the experience and helping the team improve their concepts.

SUPP

SERVICE PRINCIPLES

Workbook: Supporting materials

Now it is time to revisit the co-generated concepts, improve them, and mash them up.

Service principles are the drivers behind the users' co-designed ideas, their essence, and reasons why they exist.

They are meant to set the boundaries on what is relevant, keeping the development process aligned with users' needs and desires.

Extracting the principles.

1) Gather the ideas created during the Humanize::Perspectives step and combine the similar ones, grouping them together in small batches containing things that seem to address the same issue, were created under the same premises, or work in a similar fashion.

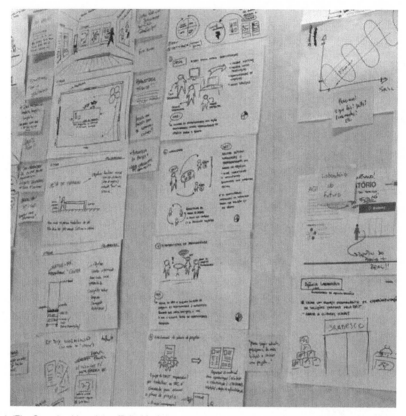

Photo/Fig: Grouping ideas into affinity blocks.

2) Give a memorable title to each of the groups. Try to use fun inspirational names, avoiding functional and boring titles like "Go shopping."

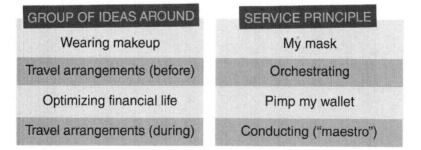

GROUP OF IDEAS AROUND	SERVICE PRINCIPLE
Wearing makeup	My mask
Travel arrangements (before)	Orchestrating
Optimizing financial life	Pimp my wallet
Travel arrangements (during)	Conducting ("maestro")

Photo/Fig: Examples around cosmetics, travel and financial projects.

Each of the group titles will serve from now on as a service principle. They will work as pointers to specific knowledge areas where opportunities to build something that helps users are present.

3) Now it is design time! Ideate with your team possible solutions within the boundaries of the service principles. Remember, at this stage you should simultaneously be working on previous user-generated content and also new ideas.

E.g.

Looking at the actual ideas under each service principle, the team should start asking:

- How can we create or mash-up ideas in order to help people better experience "My Mask"?

- How can we create or mash-up ideas in order to help people better experience "Orchestrating"?

- How can we create or mash-up ideas in order to help people better experience "Pimp my wallet"?

- How can we create or mash-up ideas in order to help people better experience "Conducting"?

From this point on, when creating new ideas, always refer to the service principles. This is useful in order to make sure the team's final solution is on track with the user's value perception field.

In the end, a set of service principles may mature to become a strong representation of the organizational scope to serve its customers, and, as such, they can turn into a good source of inspiration for the creation of a set of cultural core values.

For culture-driven organizations like Zappos, Disney and Starbucks, core values are a strong avatar of their organizational culture. Those values are ubiquitous in the workplace and presented in such a way to foster comprehension and adoption, inspiring employee behaviors at all organizational levels.

Photo/Fig: Disney's four keys. The photo shows their core values crystallized into an exclusive, employees-only set of pins.

THE MVS JOURNEY

Workbook: The MVS Journey

Target: mvs (minimum, valuable, service)

Now it is time to document the final user journey and discuss the implementation possibilities with your team and final users. It is also time to compromise, giving up on some features in order to reach a viable implementation stage. Welcome to the MVS Journey workbook, the final workbook.

Using the MVS journey workbook:

1) Write down the moments that define your service journey.

E.g.

Discover, Sign-in freemium, freemium engagement, Sign-in premium ...

2) Intention & avatars

In this space, for each moment, define all the intentions the user may express while using the service. Intentions are things the user may want to accomplish while interacting with the service. For example, the user may want to: get help, invite a friend, send a message, delete an account, or pay a fee. Make sure you focus only on the "What."

Around the user's intention, define the avatars needed for the user to accomplish what they intend to do. This is the "How." Avatars can take the form of people, processes, channels, digital manifestations or objects.

interaction = intention + avatar

When an intention ("what") meets an avatar ("how"), an interaction is triggered.

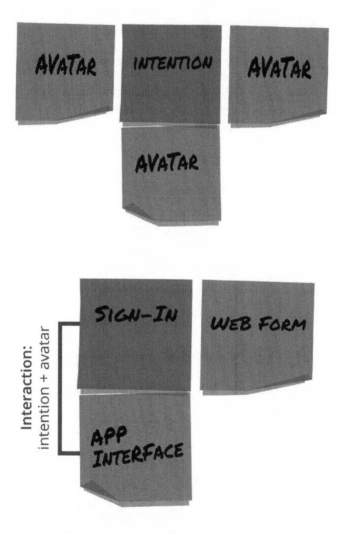

Fig: The user intention is to "Sign-in." A possible user interaction is "Sign-in via App interface."

Below you can see how intentions and avatars go together in the MVS journey. Gray Post-it notes represent the journey moments. In pink you will find the user's intentions. In blue, the avatars.

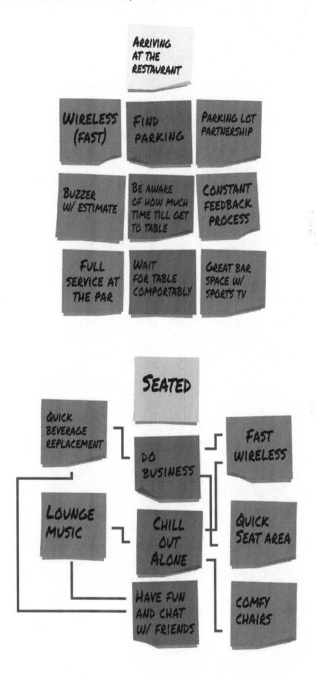

FOR THE SERVICE DESIGN ENTHUSIAST

This approach is different from the standard service blueprint, which has channels on the Y-axis, with moments on the X-axis and user intentions repeated between lanes.

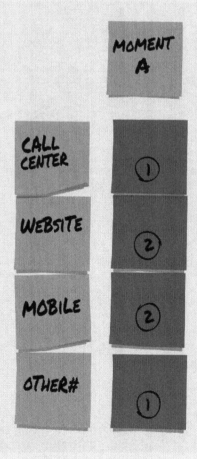

Photo/Fig: A scheme for a traditional service blueprint.

In the figure, you can see the structure of a traditional service blueprint. On the left, each swim-lane holds a channel, while in the columns the service moments are described. Users' intentions that are cross-channel appear repeated between lanes, cloaked within the events descriptions represented by the numbers in the figure.

E.g.

The moment is: First use.

The user intention is: Get help.

Call center -> Calls for instructions.

Website -> Browse for instructions.

Mobile -> Fiddle around for instructions.

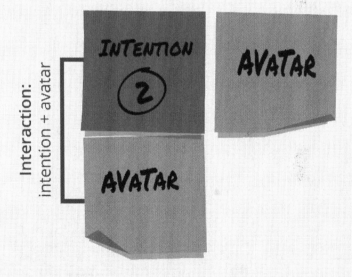

Photo/Fig: The MVS Journey.

In the picture above, you can see that the MVS journey proposes a different approach, focusing on intentions and avatars, with interactions being a result of the collision between the two.

In the MVS, an intention is only expressed once per moment, with its avatars wrapped around it. If it were a line of code, it would look exactly like parameters in a procedure call.

E.g.

The moment is: First use.

The user intention is: Get help.

_get Help [website, call center, mobile];

The MVS journey eliminates the Y-axis, steering the focus from channels to user's intentions.

This format keeps the team focused on users' behaviors. It is also helpful in situations where the team wants to describe lots of different webpages or app screens as avatars addressing the same user intention. That could be a hassle using the traditional service blueprint model.

Keep in mind that, round after round, we are focused on getting to the ideal minimum amount of avatars crucial for the first implementation round. This is why there is need to focus on the "what" (intention), separating it from the "how" (avatars). The MVS journey is a lean, WYSIWYG (what you see is what you get) blueprint that helps making the user's expectations clear. The team can then work on optimizing the avatars without inadvertently leaving users' intentions unattended.

Photo/Fig: Startup at Eise working on their service journey..

SUPP

PLAYBACK

Workbook: Supporting materials

Playback is an original form of improvisational theatre in which audience or group members tell stories from their lives and watch them enacted on the spot. The first playback theatre company was founded in 1975 by the improvisational theatre student and activist Jonathan Fox.

In the MVS, Playback is an experience prototyping session, a secure environment for the team to enact the service, in which mistakes are allowed and the project team is protected to work those mistakes out alongside with users.

Photo/Fig: An snail-mail box for patients. An experience prototype of a new service designed by Parsons students for the MSK cancer treatment center in New York.

Let's playback.

1) Take a good look at your MVS Journey and choose the interactions (intentions + avatars) you want to prototype.

2) For each interaction, write down questions that you feel are relevant and need to be answered.

3) Plan your prototype media. This can range from foam mock-ups to role-play scripts. Anything goes, as long as it is useful to simulate the service interaction.

Be wise when choosing the type of media you use for building your experience prototypes. A good media is one that triggers the user to **immerse and respond**. Do not get too fancy with the mock-ups; that usually backfires and prevents collaboration, this is because users are often less inclined to risk messing up with beautifully crafted artifacts.

That being said, your prototype needs to be credible and should help the users **immerse and respond**. Aim for functional and responsive materials.

Photo/Fig: A piece of paper serving as a prototyping media to help the project team test the time spent in line in a touch-screen terminal.

4) Invoke your hero-like users and add some average users to the mix.

5) Give them their playback routines. These are plots containing roles and goals. Sit back, watch, register and learn.

Photo/Fig: An experience prototyping session around mobility for the city of São Paulo.

After the user's performances, find the time to ask them questions like:

- So, how do you think it went? ... Why do you think so? And why is that?

- Does the service help you in any way? ... How? And why is that?

- I took a note that says: "could not easily find the card slot." Does this reflect what happened? ... Interesting... and why is that? ...

- Now... looking back to what you just experimented, tell me what do you consider the highest and lowest points in using the service? ... Interesting, why?

- Let's assume for a second you are the designer of this service, what would you do differently? ... Why?... Tell me more about this...

Hint:

A playback session is a co-design step. That means proposals here are still on the making. Make sure you have the agenda to sit with the participants to discuss ways to improve, change and create around the proposals.

Adjust and update the MVS journey workbook with what you have learned.

Play wisely. Do not overcrowd your prototype sessions. Do more sessions if you need to in order to keep up with smaller groups. Also be keen when mixing investors or high-ranking executives with customer-facing or low-level employees—some tensions may arise and you may have to balance it back.

CRYSTALLIZE :: POLISH OFF

Now it is time to wrap up and refine the concept into a viable solution. Get ready to build your "go to market" pilot.

Crystallize::Polish off is the step where you will create the build backlog for the MVS, craft the pitch and formalize the action plan.

THE BUILD BACKLOG

Workbook: The MVS Journey

To Scrum practitioners*, the Sprint backlog is the list of tasks to be completed over the next sprint, "sprint" meaning the next development cycle.

In the MVS, the Build backlog represents something similar. It is the list of avatars that will be built into the Minimum Valuable service.

In order to build a viable, feasible backlog, the project team needs to perform a trade-off between functionalities that are crucial to the pilot and attributes that are to be removed for the sake of simplification and/or viability.

In the MVS, a service can have three types of avatars:

- **Threshold:** Avatars that customers need in order to access the service.

- **Performance:** Avatars that are not absolutely necessary, but bring convenience and make the service more comfortable.

- **Excitement:** Delight avatars.

Polish it off into a minimum valuable service.

1) With the MVS journey, take a look at each possible intention and its supporting avatars. Discuss with the team, in a scale ranging from 0 to 10, the amount of effort (time and money) needed to implement each avatar.

Then discuss, in a scale ranging from 0 to 10, the amount of positive impact it will have upon the customer experience.

Add those values on a small Post-it note and place it somewhere around the avatar.

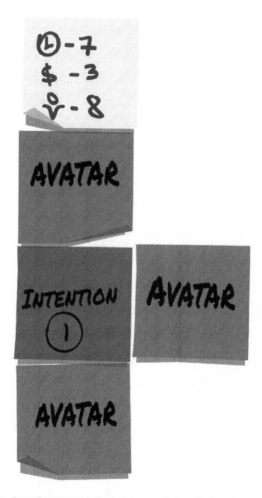

Photo: Feel free to add any other refinement variable that you may feel applies to your project.

2) For each quantified avatar, write a Post-it note, mentioning its name, and classify it in the workbook as Threshold, Performance or Excitement. Also, play around with the intentions and avatars, sending some to the waste container of the workbook. Wasted intentions are possible user motives that will not be addressed in this round of the MVS. In the same

way, wasted avatars are service evidences that will not be crystallized at this time.

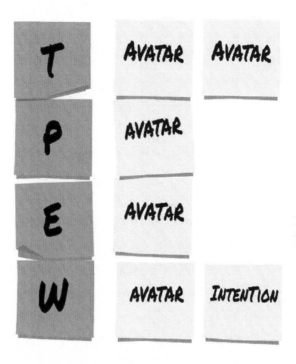

Photo/Fig: This is how your build backlog should look.

For each item that goes to the waste container, update the MVS journey's intentions and avatars area in order to reflect the new decision. Do not throw away any information; just move discarded items to the waste container and leave it there for now.

Hints:

- Make sure your minimum service has all the appropriate Threshold Attributes. If necessary, cut out Performance or Excitement Attributes so you can accommodate the Threshold Attributes.

- Select appropriate Performance Attributes so that you can deliver a service that meets users' standards at a price the customer is prepared to pay, while still maintaining a good profit margin.

- Remember you are not planning the entire service ecosystem, but a round of development that will launch a minimum service. Mind the fact that intentions that were not addressed or avatars that were left out can be incorporated later. Be brave: make the cut.

The items that you have on the Threshold, Performance or Excitement areas are the Build Backlog, the list of avatars that are needed to crystallize and bring to life your minimum valuable service.

Note: Scrum is an Agile approach to development, focused on fast sprints and small incremental iterations.

Photo/Fig: This is how your MVS journey should look.

THIS IS A GOOD TIME TO ESTIMATE YOUR SERVICE'S MARKET POTENTIAL

Sometimes it helps if you get to a clearer picture regarding the potential of the market you are trying to enter.

Considering Today and Tomorrow on the Time Machine workbook, do the math according to the explanations on the Market Potential sheet of the workbook and uncover the market potential for the solution.

In the "Today" part, you should consider the potential regarding the MVS. In the "Tomorrow" part, the exercise should be about the scalability potential for the evolved service.

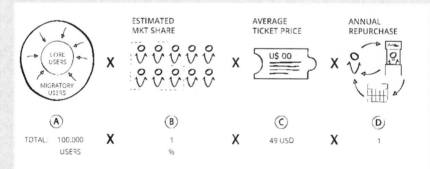

BMG CANVAS INTEGRATION
Workbook: The MVS Journey

If you like using the Business Model Generation canvas to specify a formal business plan, then you should by now have enough information to properly complete it on your own.

I will not cover the BMG canvas here, but you can find information about how to operate it on the internet or in the book *Business Model Generation*, by Alex Osterwalder.

Make sure to integrate the MVS journey with the BMG canvas by correlating the journey's intentions and avatars with the BMG canvas information.

A word of caution:

Be aware that the BMG canvas is a tool that provides only a static, bird's-eye visualization of the service being developed. Also, be sure to note that the BMG is a tool rooted on the "make and sell" economy. Why do I say that? Two reasons:

First, it suggests a separation between the front stage (right end of the canvas) and backstage (left end), based on the Line of Visibility concept discussed in chapter six.

"The right-hand side of the canvas is the front stage. The left-hand side of the canvas is the backstage..."

— Alex Osterwalder, businessmodelalchemist.com

Also, the BMG canvas was designed with the idea that the organization can create and deliver value, which goes against the premise of the Service Dominant Logic discussed in chapter 3, one of the main influences for the creation of the MVS model.

"The value proposition building block describes the bundle of products and services that create value for a specific customer segment...

"Value propositions are delivered to the customers through communication, distribution and sales channels."

— Alex Osterwalder, *Business Model Generation*

I am against the idea of kicking off the development of a new service with the BMG Canvas. Apart from all of the reasons given in Part 1 of this book, there's also the fact that none of the amazing disruptive services we know today, and like to talk about, started with the writing of a formal business plan. That would involve too many operational assumptions, a waste of time and creative energy considering the uncertainties involved in the early stages of any business.

That being said, considering that you have constructed your MVS using the human-centered perspective offered by service design, no evil may come by filling in the Business Model Canvas. Contrary to that even, the BMG canvas exercise at this late stage may provide the project team with beneficial discussions about the hard operational structure needed to run the business.

SUPP

CARVING THE PITCH

Workbook: Supporting materials

If you can't consistently stand up for your own solution, no one will feel confident enough to invest time, emotion or money in it.

This may seem rather obvious, but in Austin's South by Southwest conference (SXSW) this year—and I'm writing this in 2014—too many startups fell into the trap of not being able to explain themselves during the event's short conversations. Take a minute to think about this: even at SXSW, this amazing and rich venue for getting the word out and networking, most founders still struggled to explain the core of their business proposals.

The questions presented in this section do not cover everything that can hit you in a real pitch, but they cover a lot and are here to help you navigate this process crafting good and consistent answers to possible investors.

Remember, by "investors" I mean a possible sponsor for your initiatives. For a corporate entrepreneur, this may translate into a C-level executive.

Photo/Fig: Eise students at the Nest GSV in Silicon Valley, CA.

Next you will find my 10 preferred topics to cover in a pitch. These are things I will look to have answered when I am either mentoring or looking to invest in a new business. You will find this chart in high resolution in the supporting materials workbook.

CARVING THE PITCH!

(1) CRAFT A COMPELLING STORY ABOUT THE TEAM'S **BACKGROUND AND PREVIOUS EXPERIENCE.** THIS NEEDS TO BE QUICK AND FOCUSED ON **SKILLS AND ACTIONS THAT SOMEHOW** *(EVEN REMOTELY)* CAN BE RELATED TO —— **THE SERVICE OFFER.** ——
THE IMPLICIT QUESTION HERE IS **WHY YOUR HISTORY BACKS YOU UP?**

(2) TELL A STORY ABOUT THE PROBLEM YOU ARE SOLVING. **WHY IS THIS A PROBLEM?** WHY DOES THIS PROBLEM NEED A SOLUTION? HOW PEOPLE HAVE BEEN AVOIDING THIS ISSUE WITHOUT HAVING ACCESS TO YOUR OFFER?

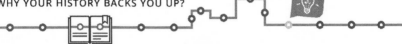

(3) *PLUS...* WHY IS YOUR SOLUTION **THE ONE THAT NAILED IT?** WHAT IS UNIQUE ABOUT WHAT |||||||||| **YOU ARE PROPOSING?** ||||||||||

HOW DOES YOUR SOLUTION RESPOND TO THE PRESENT AND WHY IS IT GOING **TO BE AROUND FOR A WHILE?** |||||||||||||||||||||||||||||||||||||||||||||||||||||||||||||||||

(4) HOW DO YOU MAKE MONEY?

(5) HOW **BIG** IS THE MARKET?

IF YOU ARE ENTERING AN ESTABLISHED MARKET, CHECK YOUR COMPETITOR'S NUMBERS. IF YOU ARE CREATING A NEW MARKET, LOOK FOR MIGRATION PATHS: CONSUMERS WILL HAVE TO COME FROM SOMEWHERE, AND THOSE PLACES ARE YOUR "COMPETITORS." IT IS ALWAYS AN AWFUL IDEA TO SAY, OR EVEN THINK, THAT BECAUSE YOUR BUSINESS IS NEW YOU HAVE NO COMPETITORS. AFTER YOUR LAUNCH, THE SALARY EARNED BY YOUR POSSIBLE CONSUMERS WILL REMAIN THE SAME AND THE TIME THAT THEY HAVE AVAILABLE TO LIVE THEIR LIVES WILL PROBABLY ALSO REMAIN THE SAME. THE REALITY IS THAT YOU ARE COMPETING FOR THOSE LIMITED ASSETS.

(6) WHO ARE YOUR COMPETITORS, AND WHO **MIGHT BECOME A COMPETITOR?** WHY ARE **YOU** GUYS BETTER POSITIONED FOR TACKLING THIS ISSUE THAN YOUR — **POSSIBLE COMPETITORS ?** —

(7) WHAT DO YOU **FEAR** THE MOST, AND WHAT COULD GO BADLY WRONG?

(8) HOW WILL **PEOPLE KNOW** YOU EXIST?

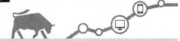

(9) IN THE FUTURE, WILL THE NATURAL PATH FOR THE STARTUP BE IPO OR M&A?

(10) WHAT IS THE LEVEL OF COMMITMENT OF THE TEAM? HOW MANY FULL-TIMERS?

GO BUILD!

     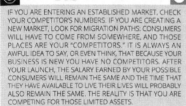 

② ③ ④	②
⑤ ⑥ ⑨	⑥

② ⑥	
④ ⑧	

SERVICE STARTUP : DESIGN GETS LEAN

theservicestartup.com

Photo/Fig: This info graphic is part of the supporting materials workbook. You can download this and other materials at **http://www.theservicestartup.com**.

GO BUILD!

Congratulations! You have just added a huge dose of design to your development process.

If you went through the steps and took the time to make some difficult choices, you should by now have in your hands a well-designed Minimum Valuable Service.

#GoBuild, #Go2Mkt and #beGood!

PIVOT OR PERSEVERE?

After the "go to market" experience you may feel like changing some features, start building others or even may pivot everything. This marks the kick-off of the next MVS round. Services are living organisms, and as such, the secret to reverse gravity (see: Eise matrix) and keeping your relevance in a service economy is to keep learning from users and applying this knowledge into the improvement of the service experience.

A good practice for minor tweaks is to move one step back into the Crystallize::Playground stage and generate new ideas based on not-yet-explored insights and connections. Or you can go two steps back into the Humanize::Perspectives and co-design new ideas with consumers. Remember that you can always remove only the sheet of the workbook containing what is being pivoted. That is the beauty of the mosaic model.

Let's say you own a new and innovative hostel, built from scratch using the MVS model. Now, as a second iteration, you decided to innovate your strategies for guest "check-in." In this case, all you have to do is go to the moment "Check-in" of the workbook "The MVS Journey," remove the pages containing the old interactions, and keep them somewhere safe. Print new workbook sheets, increment the version number in the new pages to V2.0 (or anything like it), and you are all set to work on new "check-in" possibilities for your service.

Sometimes, in a full pivot situation, a project team may want to perform another deep dive, going back all the way to Humanize::Projection. In those situations, the second round of ethnographic exploration will burn less fuel considering the knowledge already gathered during round one.

TOOLKIT

You can download the MVS workbooks at:

http://www.theservicestartup.com/Workbooks_THE_SERVICE_STARTUP.zip.

On creating it, I've dodged the plotter urge and made the workbooks based on Letter mosaics instead. The Letter format is more convenient as it is printable anywhere. It is also easy to mount, unmount and archive. This allows startup teams to use the templates at co-working spaces, or even their local Starbucks, without much hassle.

The workbooks are formatted as notebooks that expand into mosaics to stick on the wall. Their sheets are interchangeable, which means that at each new MVS round the team can opt to replace only the sheets that were modified. This makes for less material waste and generates a project documentation that is easier to expand, organize and store.

Photo/Fig: The MVS model templates were designed as Letter format mosaics.

Photo: You can also keep the results of your many rounds on the wall if you have the space. This will help you keep a good eye on your incremental changes.

All of this adds to a more organic experimentation dynamic, inviting the team to also go for small improvements in the service ecosystem, avoiding the "all or nothing" pivot trap. This is also a good reminder that, as we saw earlier in this book, in a service experience, a minor tweak in the "learn, use and remember" journey can take the user experience to a whole new level.

The extension sheets you will find in each workbook are there to help you claim more space for your Post-it notes, if needed.

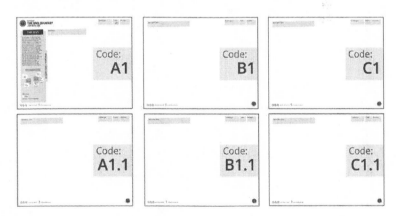

Photo: The extension sheets are, well, extensions that fit perfectly into the mosaic.

The MVS model is composed by four workbooks, plus a compendium containing supporting materials.

Last but not least, all the MVS materials are licensed as Creative Commons. They were created to be used and improved upon; just make sure to reference The Service Startup™.

THE SERVICE STARTUP BOOTCAMP

To learn how to participate or organize an edition of The Service Startup™ boot camp, go straight to http://www.theservicestartup.com, or send me an email to let me know about your interest.

The Service Startup boot camp is a hands-on experience around the MVS model. During an intense day, I take participants on a journey across a detailed tour of the MVS, including the concepts that originated it.

There are no pre-requisites to attend the Service Startup boot camp other than curiosity and a wild entrepreneurial spirit.

To learn more about the Service Startup boot camp, go to www.theservicestartup.com or reach me at tenny@theservicestartup.com.

CONCLUSION

"I think we are not in Kansas anymore," Dorothy said after she landed in Oz, and she remains right today.

The forces that were in place to shape the commercial practices during the 20th century were completely transformed by the thunderstorm of connectivity. We were thrown into a new age and a new era, one that is powered by services and where people strive for relevance instead of variety.

The old marketing school of thought that taught us to launch offerings into the market and use brute force to make them appealing to consumers is outdated and inefficient. Sure, one can insist upon it, but will then probably waste tons of money and resources on things that don't translate into real value to customers. Organizations that continue to practice this approach today are bleeding and exposed. To make it worse, this red ocean is full of fast and furious sharks. And they know that.

The "make and sell" strategies of yesterday are crippled and unable to perform smoothly in this new economy. Similarly, the scientific approach alone is unable to provide enough variety and human empathy for a business to stay relevant to the people it is meant to serve.

Yes, we live in a service economy—sadly, a collapsed one. To mention a Metallica song, our three primary mass-service structures are broken, beaten and scarred.

Our educational system was designed to prepare workers to perform basic operations at factories. The standardization of school programs was not by accident, but an intentional plan designed to create an infinite pool of human resources ready to be extracted by industries. Schools were designed to function exactly like factories, with our children treated as its raw materials.

Urban mobility services were originally designed to help factory workers commute to their jobs in the cities and to support production distribution. Nowadays, what factories? The future points to people printing their own stuff, and the remaining industrial facilities are not located in the main urban centers anymore. So why do we still commute in the same way factory workers did in 1900?

The healthcare service was created during the early industrial days. The idea was to scale health in order to extend it to the fast-growing urban population. The system was designed using scientific approaches as a foundation, and the hospital was conceived to function like a factory, only with more white and you riding the production belt.

Every startup is fueled by a rebellious instinct against the status quo. The main purpose of being small and still entering a market is to disrupt it, and propose a new and improved way to do things. In order to be successful in doing that, startups should not mirror our smoky, industrial past and rely only on scientific approaches to production. That would be to insist on repeating the same mistakes that brought us here.

The Lean Startup movement made it clear that startups need to move fast and keep waste at a minimum. However, it lacks empathy-building and co-design practices, the two main ingredients to orchestrating services that are more human, sustainable and adapted to survival in today's economy.

As we can see by historical analysis, the scientific approach alone is not capable of feeding those attributes. In order to do that, you will need design.

However, I am not talking here about the same model of engagement practiced by design agencies over the past few decades. This traditional, big account-oriented approach makes it very difficult for startups to engage and benefit from design.

I am talking about a new engagement model, one that is fast-paced and structured for constant learning. Not only that, but a model that democratizes design, allowing everyone to apply its thinking to the development of human-centric solutions.

The MVS model opens space for startups to instill design into their fast-paced development cycles. It was designed to help project teams avoid bad development decisions by integrating empathy immersions, co-design and early prototyping practices into their making.

In the MVS::Humanize mood, the team runs through generative stages where they deep dive into users' perspectives and co-design projections with them. In the MVS::Crystallize mood, the project team moves into the refinement stages. This is where they give their projections a good reality check, testing them against real-world variables and improving them along with users throughout early experience-prototyping sessions.

After a full MVS round, the project team ends up with a clear Build Backlog composed of a minimum offer forged in alignment with users' uncovered needs, desires and mental models. This better informs the development of the solution, fostering assertiveness and therefore minimizing waste.

My wish is that the concepts and tools presented in this book help you better navigate the uncertainties of developing solutions in the actual complex soup of problems and collapsed systems our society faces. The

MVS was created to help startups craft services that are relevant, perceived as meaningful, and help people live and work better.

Onward!
Tenny Pinheiro

SERVICE AS POWER

The article that follows is an academic contribution by Mauricio Manhães. It was written to be published in this book as part of his PhD research on the intersection between design, knowledge and service.

Mauricio is a good friend with whom I enjoy long and rich conversations around service innovation. He is also a co-worker at Livework. His academic contributions have been an important asset to the service design community worldwide. As he would have put it, this a "no safety net" article. It advances the concepts written on chapter 3 to synchronize them with the latest academic discoveries and publications on the subject.

Knowledge is Power. This famous phrase, which in that exact form was first written by Thomas Hobbes in 1651, is claimed by several cultures to mean that knowledge augments the power of one's own acts. The more an entity knows, the more power will have its acts on the world that surrounds it. And most of these acts of power made by an entity can be described as actions to create benefits to itself or to another. In other words, these acts can be described as service.

The whole world economy is based on service provision. Nowadays it is widely accepted that service is the fundamental basis of economic exchange: "All economies are service economies" (Vargo & Lusch, 2008). Since innovation is understood as the main driving force behind the economic growth of businesses and regions, service innovation is gaining more and more interest among corporative managers. But before organizations can create knowledge about service innovation to develop new and innovative services, first it is necessary that they understand what a service is.

Although service is everywhere, its definition is not a commonplace challenge. The simplest definition of service is: Service is something that is done to an entity by itself or another; to make it be, or feel better off after than before (Grönroos, 2008, 2011; Manhães, 2010).

A more "logical" definition is presented by the Service-Dominant Logic (SDL), describing service as the "the application of competences (such as knowledge and skills) by one party for the benefit of another" (Vargo,

Maglio, & Akaka, 2008). What is common to several of these essays of definitions is the notion of a relationship between determined potential actions and potential benefits, i.e. that a potential action can be made by an entity to attain a potential benefit for the same entity or another. The process to go from (a) potential acts to (b) fulfilled perceptions of benefits occurs as a co-creation process of value. Thus, the value co-created through the combined efforts of entities (Vargo et al., 2008) has to be perceived by the beneficiaries as value. And what is value if not knowledge, in the sense that value as knowledge must be 'tied-down' to the truth.

Otherwise, if it is not true, value would be a misunderstanding or a fraud. Thus, the value that results from a service provision has to be knowledge.

If service is understood as a knowledge creation process, it also can be said that the main goal of a service is to increase the capacity to act of an entity. Thus, service as an offering can be thought of as a (i) potential to act toward realizing a (ii) determined potential benefit. Both potentials can be completely, partially or not fulfilled at all during the realization of the related action. But, in any one of these cases, the objective of every service proposition is to realize at least these two determined potentials of: an action and a benefit.

When a set of potential acts starts to be executed, the perception of the benefits starts to become observable by the involved entities. A determined service is realized only when a final action is done, thus creating the perception by one or more entities that a proposed potential came to be realized. In other words, service is a determined set of information that supports effective actions to create a determined benefit, which correspond to the definition of knowledge as "information effective in action, information focused on results" (Drucker, 1993). In that context, knowledge is altogether information while effectively supporting a potential human action towards obtaining a determined result. This definition echoes the notion of knowledge as a dynamic "capacity-to-act" (Sveiby, 2001, p. 345).

The end of a service provision occurs when the resulting benefits are perceived by entities as fulfilled by a determined set of realized actions. The locus where the perception of benefit occurs indicates to whom the service was provided. As the value (knowledge) is co-created, the perception of benefit can be different for each one of the entities involved in the provision. Thus, it can occur that the "provider" perceives greater value than the "receiver" of a particular service, or vice-versa. Which means that it is not always clear who is serving and who is being served. This dubious perception creates an enormous amount of creative energy to develop new and radically innovative service.

In that sense, service can be understood as a social construction to improve one's own potential capacity-to-act. Plato's (c.427–347 BC) notion of knowledge as a socially "justified true belief" (Jensen, Johnson, Lorenz, & Lundvall, 2007) integrated with its definition "as potential rather than actuality" (Krogh, Takeuchi, Kase, & Canton, 2013, p. 4) helps to draw a clearer place of service into the knowledge spectrum, which could support the understanding that service is the application of intangible assets for improve the potential capacity-to-act of oneself or others. If every service is a potential do act that can be co-created; and knowledge is defined as potential to act; then, service can be defined as a knowledge creation process.

Every service proposition is as a cognitive prosthesis, through which an entity should realize its potential to act to obtain a particular set of benefits. Be that done to its own benefit or also to the benefit of another, in both cases, a service is a social process in which (i) information, (ii) effective action and (iii) a specific set of benefits are integrated to co-create knowledge, i.e. value.

Based on the reasoning above, the most important question an organization has to answer towards create innovative service is:

What knowledge our customers do co-create with us?

In other words, the focus of that question is on what is the power an organization co-creates with and, simultaneously, to its customers. The effort is to understand what capacity-to-act a company increases to its customers. The answer to that question is definitely the most powerful knowledge an organization can gain from its customers.

Mauricio Manhães

Gregório Varvakis, PhD

UFSC

REFERENCES

CHAPTER 1

Laszlo Moholy Nagy, The New vision fundamentals of Bauhaus Design, Painting, Sculpture and Architecture, 1938.

Daniel Bell, The coming of post-industrial society. A venture in Social Forecasting, 1976.

McKinsey&Company: The consumer decision journey:
http://www.mckinsey.com/insights/marketing_sales/the_consumer_decisio n_journey

Bruce Nussbaum Design Thinking is a failed experiment so whats next. http://www.fastcodesign.com/1663558/design-thinking-is-a-failed-experiment-so-whats-next

Fordism, Wikipedia, http://en.wikipedia.org/wiki/Fordism.

McKinsey&Company: The Human factor in Service Design http://www.mckinsey.com/insights/operations/the_human_factor_in_servic e_design

CHAPTER 2

Jeffrey K. Liker, The Toyota Way: 14 Management Principles from the World's Greatest Manufacturer

Lean enterprise institute. A Brief history of Lean, online article can be found at: https://www.lean.org/WhatsLean/History.cfm

The Economist. The MBAs, some history.
http://www.economist.com/node/2135907

Rachel Botsman. What's mine is yours - The Rise of Collaborative Consumption, 2010.

Society for Human Resource Management, Dress & Appearance: Tattoos/Piercings: Can employers have dress code requirements that prohibit all tattoos and piercings? Online essay can be found at: http://www.shrm.org/TemplatesTools/hrqa/Pages/tattoosandpiercings.aspx

CHAPTER 3

Satmetrix, Net Promoter Benchmarking, netpromoter.com/why-net-promoter/compare/.

Daniel Kahneman, Thinking fast and slow, 2011.

Nielsen Group, Global Trust in Advertising and Brand Messages, 2013.

Tony Hsieh's, Delivering Happiness: A Path to Passion, Profits and Purpose, 2010.

Vargo and Lusch, Evolving to a new Dominant Logic for marketing, 2004.

Lynn Shostack, Journal of Marketing, "Breaking Free From Product Marketing", 1977.

CHAPTER 5

"Virtue rewarded: Helping others at work makes people happier" University of Wisconsin-Madison News, July 29, 2013 http://www.news.wisc.edu/21983

Leonard L Berry. Discovering the soul of service, the nine drivers of sustainable business success, 1999.

Jeremy Rifkin, The Age of Access: The New Culture of Hypercapitalism Where All of Life Is a Paid-For Experience, 2000.

Service Design, wikipedia, http://en.wikipedia.org/wiki/Service_design

CHAPTER 6

Neil McBride, Centre for IT Service Management, De Montfort University, Where is your line of visibility? - http://www.cse.dmu.ac.uk/~nkm/PAPERS/Where%20is%20your%20line%20of%20visibility.pdf

Edgar Schein, Organizational culture and Leadership, John Wiley & Sons, Mar 24, 2006.

Tennyson Pinheiro, Core 77, http://www.core77.com/blog/columns/meta-service_design_designing_a_way_for_design_to_survive_in_a_toxic_organizational_enviroment_25095.asp

CHAPTER 7

Joseph Campbell, the Hero with a thousand faces, 1949

CHAPTER 8

Darius Mehri, The Darker Side of Lean, An Insider's Perspective on the Realities of the Toyota Production System.

http://astro.temple.edu/~rmudambi/Teaching/BA951/Week_04/Toyota-Darker-Side-Mehri.pdf

Eric Ries, The Lean Startup, how today's entrepreneurs use continuous innovation to create radically successful businesses, 2011.

**The Lean Startup is a trademark and service mark owned by Eric Ries.*

CHAPTER 10

Steve Blank, The Startup Owners Manual: The step by step guide for building a great company, 2012.

CHAPTER 11

Pat Kirkham, Charles and Ray Eames: Designers of the Twentieth Century, 1998.

The Design Council UK, Managing Design in eleven global brands. https://www.designcouncil.org.uk/sites/default/files/asset/document/Eleven Lessons_Design_Council%20(2).pdf

CHAPTER 13

Design Index: The Impact of Design on Stock Market Performance. http://pinkfroginteractive.com/downloads/design_index_9199.pdf?Page/@id=6049&Session/@id=D_5AFITvf705tL9HUtNzYb&Document/@id=6923

CHAPTER 14

Usability studies and the Hawthorne effect, Ritch Macefield, Staffordshire University, http://www.usabilityprofessionals.org/upa_publications/jus/2007may/hawthorne-effect.pdf

Jakob Nielsen, Thinking Aloud: The #1 Usability Tool, http://www.nngroup.com/articles/thinking-aloud-the-1-usability-tool/

The Kano Model, Understanding the Kano Model, a tool for sophisticated designers https://www.uie.com/articles/kano_model/

SERVICE IS POWER

Grönroos, C. (2008). Service logic revisited: who creates value? And who co-creates? European Business Review, 20(4), 298–314. doi:10.1108/09555340810886585

Grönroos, C. (2011). Value co-creation in service logic: A critical analysis. Marketing Theory, 11(3), 279–301. doi:10.1177/1470593111408177

Jensen, M. B., Johnson, B., Lorenz, E., & Lundvall, B. Å. (2007). Forms of knowledge and modes of innovation. Research Policy, 36(5), 680–693. doi:10.1016/j.respol.2007.01.006

Krogh, G. von, Takeuchi, H., Kase, K., & Canton, C. G. (2013). Towards Organizational Knowledge. (G. von Krogh, H. Takeuchi, K. Kase, & Cã©. GonzÃ¡lez CantÃ3n, Eds.)Towards Organizational Knowledge: The Pioneering Work of Ikujiro Nonaka (p. 384). Palgrave Macmillan. doi:10.1057/9781137024961

Manhães, M. C. (2010). Innovation in Services and the Knowledge Creation Process: a proposal a service design method. Federal University of Santa Catarina - Brazil.

Sveiby, K. (2001). A knowledge-based theory of the firm to guide in strategy formulation. Journal of Intellectual Capital, 2(4), 344–358. doi:10.1108/14691930110409651

Vargo, S. L., & Lusch, R. F. (2008). Service-dominant logic: continuing the evolution. Journal of the Academy of Marketing Science, 36(1), 1–10.

Vargo, S. L., Maglio, P. P., & Akaka, M. (2008). On value and value co-creation: A service systems and service logic perspective. European Management Journal, 26(3), 145–152. doi:10.1016/j.emj.2008.04.003

ABOUT THE AUTHOR

Tenny Pinheiro lives in San Francisco, CA. He is the author of three books on Design Thinking and Service Design, his latest publications are called The Service Startup: Design Thinking gets Lean and Breaking Free From The Lean Startup Religion: The Service Designer Manifesto. Both covering the intersection between service design and entrepreneurship.

Tenny is the founder and former CEO of the Brazilian office of the pioneer global service design agency Livework, and the founder of the service-design for all initiative Servicedesignsprints.com. Tenny is also the founder of EISE, the School for Service Innovation a pioneer educational program which accelerates entrepreneurship through service design.

He advises and consults for Fortune 500 companies, NGOs and governmental agencies, and writes a service design column for Core 77.

Practical, strategic, and respected, Tennyson brings his unique cultural perspective and experience to the table. This Brazilian serial entrepreneur and one-time resident of post-war Angola, for whom he designed government services, understands the challenges of navigating cultural complexities and the need to be adaptive, adept, and agile. A pragmatic optimist, Tennyson believes there is always something one can do, something to be done, and that what is essential is the "doing."

http://www.eiselab.com

http://www.servicedesignsprints.com

http://www.theservicestartup.com

http://about.me/tennydesign

http://www.tennypinheiro.com

http://www.twitter.com/tennydesign

I hope you have enjoyed this book. Now, it is time to put the MVS model to use and make sure you let me know about your results. =)

#goSprint #serviceDesignSprints

Tenny Pinheiro.

Made in the USA
Lexington, KY
17 September 2015